UNSHAKABLE
LEADERSHIP

UNSHAKABLE
LEADERSHIP

A Map For Unlocking
Strength, Strategy, And Success

JANET KENDALL WHITE

INDIE BOOKS
INTERNATIONAL

UNSHAKABLE **LEADERSHIP**
A Map For Unlocking Strength, Strategy, And Success

ISBN 13: 978-1-966168-39-3
Library of Congress Control Number: 2025917279

Designed by Melissa Farr, Back Porch Creative, LLC

INDIE BOOKS INTERNATIONAL®, INC.
2511 WOODLANDS WAY
OCEANSIDE, CA 92054
www.indiebooksintl.com

Contents

Preface

Leadership is not a destination; it is a lifelong journey of growth, discovery, and resilience. This book is the culmination of decades spent in the trenches—coaching executives, facilitating leadership development, and helping organizations navigate the complexities of an ever-changing world. It is built on hard-earned experience, practical application, and a deep passion for learning.

I am, at my core, a learning junkie. I have spent years studying leadership in all its forms, drawing insights from the greatest minds in the field—researchers, thought leaders, and practitioners who have shaped our understanding of what it means to lead effectively. Their work has influenced my own, and this book stands on the shoulders of those who came before me.

Yet, leadership is not just theory—it is action. Every concept, tool, and technique in these pages has been tested in real-world scenarios, refined through trial and success, and adapted to meet the needs of modern leaders. I have seen firsthand what works, what doesn't, and what makes a lasting impact.

This book is not about quick fixes or trendy leadership fads. It is about building the kind of leadership that endures—leadership that is rooted in emotional intelligence, clear communication, and the ability to navigate complexity with confidence. Whether you are an emerging leader or a seasoned executive, my goal is to provide you with practical strategies that elevate your leadership and help you build a more resilient, high-performing team.

As you embark on this journey, know that you are not alone. Leadership is not a solitary endeavor—it is a shared experience of learning, adapting, and growing. I invite you to engage fully, apply these insights to your own leadership practice, and continue the lifelong pursuit of becoming the leader you were meant to be.

Let's get started.

Janet Kendall White
Cuyahoga Falls, Ohio

PART I

Leading Through Turbulence:
Strategies For Uncertain Times

You may think that expenses like rent, cost of goods, or technology have the biggest impact on your bottom line. According to a survey cited by PeopleKeep,[1] US businesses that experience turnover also see nearly $2 trillion in lost productivity costs. This only tracks costs from when the employee actually leaves, and that employee is most certainly not at 100 percent productivity all the way up until that departure point.

Following a period of growth in prior years, US employee engagement experienced its first yearly decrease in ten years, falling from 36 percent of workers being engaged in 2020 to 34 percent in 2021.

This downward trend persisted through 2022, with only 32 percent of full-time and part-time employees at organizations now showing engagement, while 18 percent demonstrate active disengagement. Active disengagement rose by two percentage points since 2021 and four points since 2020.

The proportion of engaged versus actively disengaged workers in the US stands at 1.8 to 1, down from 2.1 to 1 in 2021 and 2.6 to 1 in 2020. This represents the smallest ratio of engaged to actively disengaged employees in the US since 2013, nearly ten years ago. The highest ratio on record was 2.7 to 1 in 2019.[2]

Gallup assesses employee engagement through surveys of random working population samples, examining specific workplace factors that correlate with various organizational outcomes, including profitability, productivity, customer relations, employee retention, workplace safety, and overall well-being. Throughout 2022, Gallup administered quarterly surveys to the working population, comprising random samples of approximately 15,000 full-time and part-time US workers each quarter. The findings presented represent an average of these four quarterly results.

The survey evaluates various workplace factors, including how much employees agree on having clear expectations, access to growth opportunities, and feeling their perspectives matter at work. Simply put, engaged workers are committed to and passionate about their roles and the organization. Actively disengaged workers are dissatisfied and uncommitted due to unaddressed workplace needs.[3, 4, 5]

Employees are now expecting more from their leaders. They want to feel heard, appreciated, and rewarded, which they have always wanted—now, that's nonnegotiable. The leaders of the past can no longer rest on their laurels. No matter how long you have been a leader, there is now an urgency to reflect on your own development and level up your leadership game.

CEOs are well aware of the need for a strong workforce. "C-suite leaders believe that a hybrid model, where a number of employees work together on site some of the time, will increase competition for top talent. Around 40 percent of CEOs globally also expect this model will lead to improvements in worker productivity as well as an increase in innovation capacity—long-standing goals for many CEOs.

"Yet survey responses indicate concerns that these benefits will come at the cost of the kind of relationships that build strong and successful working cultures over the long run. A majority (61 percent) believe a significant shift in corporate culture will be required for hybrid work to work well in their organizations."[6] The question then becomes, what are you shifting and why?

To have a high-performing hybrid work model, there needs to be more focus on how leaders show up and communicate. Management skills now need to be more attuned to the nuances of these hybrid groups. Over 85 percent of CEOs and senior executives believe the model necessitates greater emphasis on modern leadership effectiveness.

To retain top talent, organizations are re-recruiting their teams, offering a compelling new vision, and recognizing the dedication shown during challenging times. However, if you are asking who opened the barn doors after the horses escaped, you are too late. Employees have been sharing their discontent with leadership for a long time. The new focus should be to do a checkup from the neck up. And that checkup starts with you.

> Employees have been sharing their discontent with leadership for a long time. The new focus should be to do a checkup from the neck up. And that checkup starts with you.

This book is designed to assist you with your checkup. Leadership has moved into a new era. If you are not preparing to invest in your leadership skills and move into this new era, it won't just leave you behind—it will run you over.

1

Employees Are Refusing To Return To What Was— And So Should You

---

If there's one thing that's certain in business, it's uncertainty.
STEPHEN COVEY

The pandemic has irrevocably altered the work landscape. Employees have experienced the flexibility, autonomy, and balance that remote work can offer, and there's no turning back. The old paradigms have shifted, and leaders must embrace this change to foster a resilient and engaged workforce.

The past several years have continued to bring about profound changes in how we work, think, and live. The pandemic acted as a catalyst for many of these transformations, accelerating trends that were already underway and highlighting the need for adaptability and resilience. As we move forward, these changes will continue to shape the future of work and society.

I have introduced the following five new realities into the conversation. These have forever shifted the methodology of how and where we work. I have identified these critical modifications from research done over three decades, including training several thousand participants in my programs and assessing over two thousand using the Everything DiSC assessment.

The first step to leveling up your leadership game is to understand how the playing field has been forever altered. These new realities need to be taken into consideration because your employees have changed their expectations of your skills.

New Reality Number One: Remote Work And Hybrid Models

Shift To Remote Work

Following the pandemic, we have seen a sudden and widespread shift to remote work. Many companies adopted remote work policies almost overnight, leading to a reevaluation of traditional office environments. If there is now a desire to shift back to in-office working, be sure to fully explore the rationale for this shift. In addition, it is critical to communicate the why and the how behind coming back to work in the office.

Another area that can cause this modification to go off the rails is inconsistency in the adoption of remote or in-office work environments. Nothing is worse than one manager following corporate policies regarding in-office engagement and requiring their employees to return to the office, while some or all of the remaining managers decide to let employees work remotely. Be consistent with changes.

Studies have shown that in-office workers tend to have an environment that supports creativity and produce at a higher rate, not because they are not at home, but because there are more opportunities for collaboration.[7] Economics is driving a push for remote work, and technology supports it. However, if your projects have better results when everyone is in the room, then discuss why and how the in-office environment will work in the new normal.

Leaders navigating hybrid environments are operating in a landscape filled with ambiguity. With limited visibility into team workloads and workflows, and fewer chances for spontaneous, two-way conversations, many struggle to maintain a clear sense of progress and control. At the same time, they face the challenge of fostering cohesion, collaboration, and camaraderie—hallmarks of in-person work—while also promoting the flexibility and autonomy that remote work provides. As a result, their ability to lead effectively is under pressure. This has led to a growing emphasis on developing strategies specifically designed for leading in hybrid settings.[8]

Hybrid Work Models

As pandemic restrictions lifted, many organizations transitioned to hybrid work models that blend remote and in-office work. Whether individuals were involved in shaping this shift or not, it has had a significant impact on workplace culture, communication practices, and the measurement of productivity. However, emerging research indicates that hybrid models often yield the lowest productivity outcomes compared to fully remote or entirely on-site arrangements.[9] Managing both remote and in-person meetings with a video component can be tricky at the best of times. It is easy to only focus on the people in the room.

Other studies have shown that individuals who participate virtually in a hybrid meeting tend to share less, have less impact on the group, and miss opportunities to showcase skill sets that could aid their career growth.[10] This does not mean that hybrid work models should be abandoned, but understanding the ramifications and costs of this modification and taking measures to alleviate the issues are important.

Leadership Takeaway

Set clear, measurable goals and give employees the trust, responsibility, and authority to meet them.

New Reality Number Two: Technological Advancements

Acceleration Of Digital Transformation

During the past several years, businesses accelerated their digital transformation efforts to support remote work and digital customer interactions. Cloud computing, cybersecurity, and AI saw increased investment. Things are moving very fast, and even when you feel that you have caught up today, you may already be behind for the world of tomorrow.

Be comfortable when adopting technology, even if you're initially bad at it. And it's also OK not to "keep up;" you don't need to, but you do need to continue adapting. In fact, according to TechJury, the compound annual growth rate for AI is projected to be just over 42 percent by 2027.[11] That means advancements are not slowing down anytime soon.

Collaboration Tools

In recent years, the adoption of tools like Zoom, Microsoft Teams, and Slack has become ubiquitous, transforming how teams communicate and collaborate. These collaboration tools are important, even if all of your team members are in one physical location. The tools act as a notetaker and, with the use of AI, can even summarize and outline critical points of the meeting, including agreed-upon action items.

Leadership Takeaway

Technology is a tool; make it your friend to the degree that it will help with day-to-day tasks. Don't worry about getting ahead of the curve, you won't, and you don't need to. Remember, you have to be bad at it before you are good at it. If you have avoided technology in the past, you can no longer get away with that today.

New Reality Number Three: Mental Health Awareness

Increased Focus On Well-being

The pandemic highlighted the importance of mental health, with increased awareness and initiatives to support employee well-being. Companies began offering more mental health resources and flexible work options to reduce burnout.

Empathetic leaders are now needed to understand what employees might be experiencing. There still needs to be caution.

Leaders who were not so good a couple of years ago stand out as some of the worst leaders in today's world.

Burnout And Stress

Remote work blurred the boundaries between personal and professional life, leading to higher levels of stress and burnout.[12] This has prompted discussions about work-life balance and the need for mental health support. This blurring of lines can enable leaders to provide support, allowing employees to take care of themselves. However, even with knowledge of your employees' situations, you will still need to offer some tough love.

While leaders may focus solely on removing negative factors, they also need to create a positive environment. Dr. Steve Swavely, a well-known leadership neuropsychologist, shared insight based on his book, *Ignite Your Leadership*.[13] "Leaders need to now pay attention to the environment they create. And they have control to produce an environment that increases well-being, reduces burnout, limits stress, and builds engagement."

Leadership Takeaway

No one is asking you to suddenly become a therapist. What is now expected of you is to understand the impact of stress on mental health and get familiar with new approaches to helping your employees with potential burnout. If you believe employees are the business lifeblood, which they are, you need to protect that resource.

New Reality Number Four: Global Political And Social Changes And Unrest

Political Uncertainty

The past few years have seen significant political changes and uncertainties, including the rise of populist movements, geopolitical tensions, and policy shifts. These factors have affected global markets and business strategies. We sometimes experience only nasty conflict instead of productive conflict. Divisiveness needs to be rallied against.

What leaders should navigate in today's world is to understand that external change may be affecting employees and still keep the internal environment supportive and safe for diverse opinions that are shared in a respectful, constructive way.

Social Movements

Movements such as Black Lives Matter and #MeToo have brought issues of diversity, equity, and inclusion to the forefront. Companies continue to focus on creating inclusive environments and addressing systemic inequalities regardless of the initials attached to it.

This means creating a culture of inclusion, no matter the political persuasion. Model the behavior you want to see and keep a neutral work environment. As a leader, you must learn to have your personal beliefs and the beliefs of your team members coexist in the workplace.

You can share enough of yourself without being controversial and without taking away from the safe environment that you create. Your employees should be able to know who you are, especially through the lens of business. Your beliefs and values make you a unique type of leader. Those values have created the experiences that have made you this leader in this moment.

Your values and character as a leader will always be important. They affect how you lead and how others follow. You need to be aware of those aspects in your leadership and ensure there is an environment that is safe for people to fully engage with their team on the work at hand and to hold a safe crucible for diverse ideas and opinions.

Leadership Takeaway

Help your employees find and build common ground. That starts with you. Model engaging the communication and behavior you expect from others. Keep the priority focused on the business of business.

> Keep the priority focused on the business of business.

New Reality Number Five: Economic Shifts

Economic Disruption

The pandemic caused economic disruptions that have continued through to the current volatility. This includes job losses, changes in consumer behavior, and shifts in global supply chains. Companies continue to have to adapt to these changes quickly to survive.

Being adaptive to uncertainty can help your employees shift as well. They are looking at you for guidance, and resilience and calmness are traits that can be adopted by your employees to keep the company running.

Gig Economy Growth

There has been a rise in gig and freelance work as individuals seek more flexible and autonomous working arrangements. Platforms like Uber, Upwork, and Fiverr have grown in popularity. As a leader, you will have to manage non-employees at some point in your career. How much you make those contractors a component of your team will depend on how crucial their role is in the project and organization.

Culture will affect how well these 1099 workers are treated by the rest of the team. Have you explained their role and responsibilities to the rest of the group? Sharing this information can help others understand how that worker benefits the project and the team dynamics.

Leadership Takeaway

If the economic ground your employees are standing on shifts, you can be sure the same will happen to the ground your business is on. By providing strong and consistent leadership, you are also providing a safe harbor for your employees. Employees are looking for your calm guidance and level head now more than ever. Are you providing that?

How have you modified your leadership to accommodate the changes these new realities create in yourself and others?

2

How To Reach Employees Now

Just as the seasons turn, the world is shifting, adapting, and finding new roots. Embrace this new reality as the soil from which resilience and renewal will grow.

JANET KENDALL WHITE

During the lockdown portion of the pandemic, I found myself spending 100 percent of my working time in a home office that I already had but usually spent less than 30 percent of my working time in. The work I was doing also dramatically changed. The revenue that I had just worked to build evaporated in one day when the lockdown was announced. This was because I was doing in-person work and speaking. Rather than ask me if I could pivot and do it remotely, people panicked.

I salvaged a two-day training session that was scheduled right after lockdown to be in person for a leadership academy. There were approximately twenty leaders who were graduating after those two days. I rushed to make it all happen as interactively as I could using technology while they were scrambling to figure out life working at home. Coming out of those two days, I knew that life as everyone knew it had changed forever.

I realized that things would not go "back to normal" the way they had been. Others would say to me, "When things get back to normal," but I knew that with the impact of massive and required change, there would evolve a new normal. Companies were learning how to operate remotely, and also that they could save money on their hefty building leases. Employees were learning that they could have flexibility, including working from anywhere for anyone.

Shortly before the lockdown mandate, I had helped grow and sell a company. That project had been draining physically, mentally, and emotionally. There was a six-month period where I was only home for a total of five days. Suddenly, I had no travel and no work coming in. I felt like a boat with no oars, motor, or sails.

I was lost and didn't know what in the heck I wanted to do. All I saw on social media were people putting up videos of themselves. That was not something I felt comfortable doing. All my clients have come from referrals or speaking engagements.

A woman had turned me on to the Referral of a Lifetime system—one of the first steps is that you send a letter to your A-list clients.[14] I had started that, and the system says you're not going to see results for six months. And yet, one of my prior clients reached out when they received that first letter, not long after lockdown. They referred a CEO who needed help to solidify her leadership team and grow the business. That led to my ongoing life on Zoom.

Within thirty days, I found myself coaching CEOs and executives over Zoom on everything from how to manage remotely and keep people engaged to how to trust that people were being productive at home without the normal guardrail of physical oversight.

Employees struggled with children and partners/spouses at home without the space to operate dual offices or even the ability to have multiple phone calls going on at the same time. Schools struggled to pivot and handle students right away while parents attempted to work. One person I spoke to in an organization was working in their dark, unfinished basement because it was the only room she had to use. She struggled to maintain her motivation in that environment. In addition, she was working through being needed as a mom upstairs while her manager was "checking in" every five minutes to see if she was actually working.

This scenario reminds me of a conversation with one of my clients. I was performing a continuous improvement project for one of my manufacturing clients. A foreman said something that many employees were struggling with: "In high school, my coach told me what to do. In the army, my sergeant told me what to do. My boss has told me what to do, and now you are asking me to think on my own?"

This concern was amplified among many employees and leaders when the lockdown began. The safety net was sharply pulled away, and everyone was in the same boat. "How would I deal with personal issues at home?" "Where was the home office going to go?" Leaders were dealing with all these extra issues, and still had to manage employees, who were also dealing with the same types of issues. There was a level of overwhelm seldom seen in the workplace.

People had to figure out things they had never done before, ranging from technology to schooling to safety. During the lockdown, people kept saying, "I can't wait to get back to normal." And I would respond, "There is going to be a new reality. If your employees aren't going to be the same, you can't be the same leader."

It goes back to building relationships, communication, empathy, and understanding of this new paradigm. Working on relationships and empathy can help your employees regain their confidence and autonomy.

With the increasing prevalence of technology, it is essential to remember the four-stage rule for technology improvement. When you first start using new technology, you will be very slow and bad at it, compared to the old way. During the second stage, you will begin to gain proficiency and become as fast and skilled as you were with the old way. In the third stage, you will become much faster and more accurate. The fourth stage is where you move into a new level that was not possible with the old way of working.

Each stage is critical in becoming more efficient.

Actions To Take

Get Consistent

Prepared leaders take action to become more consistent. This means communicating and applying company policies and procedures to ensure that everyone understands the policies, can refer to them, and has the same experience with their implementation. It also makes life easier for you as a leader if you are clear about your own expectations including "hot buttons," and your employees have understood and agreed to them. When an issue arises and someone is not meeting expectations, it is easier to remind them if the expectations have been clearly communicated from the outset.

Practice Good Communication

Leaders need to practice good communication and look for opportunities to improve it. Be clear, be concise, and be consistent in your messaging. Communicate early and often, and assume that you will need to communicate at least two more times for the message to be fully understood. Set up time for more relaxed huddles for both in-office and remote workers.

Become More Empathetic

The third action for leaders to take is under the umbrella of empathy. Being empathetic is a vital component to leading in today's uncertain times. We all will benefit from being more human and understanding. Give grace and space to the degree you can while still maintaining performance expectations. Grace teaches us to navigate life with kindness, compassion, and elegance, while "space" reminds us of the importance of giving ourselves and others room to grow, heal, and simply be.

PART II

The LeadMap:
Charting The Course For Unshakable Leadership

Every resilient leader needs to be on this quest. It is a continuous journey, and we learn valuable lessons along the way. Though each persons journey is different, we all need a map and various tools to assist us in our journey.

A leader is never alone in this work and on this journey. We need to bring other leaders along to develop new leaders and create a network of support.

The prize includes achieving business objectives, which can be growth, developing high-performing teams, growing market share, or increasing productivity, *and* it is personal fulfillment knowing you have made a difference.

All leaders should practice the three R's of growth: receive, retain, and release. You first receive new knowledge and skills. You then work to retain that knowledge and new skills. You then release them to your colleagues and team. In medical school, they call this process see one, do one, teach one. This ties into your support system to challenge you and hold you accountable, while helping you stay on the learning journey and avoid stagnation.

The following skills and habits that you will acquire are part of my leadership development process, the LeadMap, which has been developed over decades of research and client work. I am a self-proclaimed learning junkie, and while this is not a new process, it is a refined process, bringing in the best practices of several schools of thought. It is your journey. Your tools. Your growth utilizing the LeadMap.

Nothing creams my corn or overcooks my grits more than someone claiming a revolutionary process when it really is a modification or compilation of current practices. I will not say that this is a brand-new process that everyone needs to follow. I am sharing with you what I've seen that works based on my experience and my thirst for knowledge and growth.

This map will assist you on a journey to level up skills from communication and logistics to decision-making and emotional intelligence. With mastery of the tools and skills in the LeadMap, you will become an adaptable and tenacious leader who can skillfully manage and lead your team to sustainable and consistent success.

One of the most critical responsibilities of a leader is setting clear expectations from the start. When people know what is expected of them—how they should communicate, collaborate, and operate within a team—they are far more likely to meet those expectations. Clear expectations remove ambiguity, reduce miscommunication, and create a foundation of trust. Without them, employees are left to interpret what is acceptable, which can lead to misunderstandings, inconsistent performance, and frustration on both sides.

By laying out expectations upfront, you provide a clear reference point that makes it easier to address issues when they arise. If someone is not meeting a standard, you can simply point back to the expectations that were already established, reinforcing accountability in a way that feels fair and consistent. This eliminates the need to backtrack and explain expectations after a problem has already surfaced, which can feel reactive and, at times, unfair to the person involved. Instead, a proactive approach ensures that everyone is aligned from the beginning, making leadership more effective and guidance more straightforward.

For leaders, this clarity makes it easier to lead, and for employees, it makes it easier to follow. People perform best when they understand what success looks like and how they contribute to the bigger picture. Setting expectations isn't about control; it's about empowerment. When people know the rules of engagement, they can operate with confidence, knowing that their actions align with what is expected of them. This not only fosters a stronger team dynamic but also builds a culture of accountability and mutual respect.

My Leadership Expectations

- Communication, communication, communication. Be clear, be proactive, and ensure alignment.

- Be on time. Respect others' time by being punctual for meetings and commitments.

- Keep commitments. Follow through on what you say you'll do. If you can't, communicate early.

- Ask for help when you need it. No one succeeds alone. Seeking support is a strength, not a weakness.

- Be up-front about mistakes and learn from them. Own your missteps, make corrections, and grow from the experience.

- Respect each other's contributions. Engage actively, listen attentively, and value diverse perspectives.

- Honesty and integrity are expected. Transparency and trust are non-negotiable. A lack of honesty or integrity will not be tolerated.

- Open door policy—nothing is off limits. I encourage open dialogue. If something is on your mind, let's talk about it.

This is one example that I use—you can and should create your own. An additional example of leadership expectations of a global organization leader is included in appendix C.

So, let's begin that journey with the first cornerstone: effective communication.

Increase Effective Communications

No one cares how much you know,
until they know how much you care.
OFTEN ATTRIBUTED TO THEODORE ROOSEVELT

Effective communication can make or break a leader and is foundational for a successful journey.

Here is one story of when I was the chief human resources officer, and a fellow C-level executive was let go. The details have been changed to keep confidentiality.

We had a vice president who was decent at his job. His interpersonal skills, however, became toxic. The company worked with him to help him hear this critical feedback. He just didn't get it. He was not working well with other executives and was often blaming others instead of examining what he could do differently. Even though he was earning a multi-six-figure income, he was let go. And it was not because he couldn't do his job; it was because he could not deal effectively with other people. The root cause was communication style and effectiveness, especially with those who were managed.

This flaw was vital, as it is very well known that employees don't leave their company, they leave their manager.

The Right Questions To Ask

When you think about communication, there are several things to consider.

What information do I have? Who needs to know it? Have I actually told them in a manner that makes the information clear to them?

The first step in practicing effective communication is to understand your communication style, as well as that of others. What are your personality, strengths, weaknesses, priorities, stressors, and motivators? What are theirs? You cannot adapt your communication style to someone else if you do not know, at a minimum, what your own communication style is.

The utilization of assessment tools is critical with this foundational element. They provide you with basic information to get started. While there are many leadership and communication assessment tools available, our preferred tool is the Everything DiSC suite of products. And it is preferred for a reason.

I am certified in numerous leadership development assessments and have used many over the years. I have found that for individual, team, and organizational development, the Everything DiSC resources provide great foundational tools for a baseline and future development. My apologies if this comes across as a sales pitch, and in some ways, it is—but only because I have seen the impact.

By combining self-assessments with flexible facilitation and the Catalyst online learning platform, participants experience rich aha moments that inspire lasting behavior change. It is *the* tool that we have used effectively at all levels of organizations, from the CEO to the rest. It is immediately applicable—people remember it and are able to utilize it to better understand themselves and others and to build better relationships. The lasting impact provides a high return on investment from the assessment, facilitation, and online learning system.

Sharing Information Is Only Half The Equation

You may not think about it, but effective communication also means practicing effective listening. This includes asking questions to further the conversation with a focus on understanding; being present in the conversation, whether it is in person or via email or other digital channels; and not competing to get your point across, but allowing the conversation to flow both ways.

Perhaps your best tool is to paraphrase what was shared. This causes you to implement a few skills simultaneously. First, you have to be actively present to understand what the other person is sharing. You cannot be thinking of your response. Second, you will need to be aware of the feelings of the other person to be able to capture sentiment. And third, this exercise will help you to simply reflect back an idea, with no judgment of the idea or the person.

This type of communication takes practice to progress. You will not be perfect the first time out, and that is OK. By focusing on both hearing and understanding, you will achieve better communication and bigger strides toward the end goal.

Adaptation Of Communication Styles

Once you understand your preferred communication style and the communication styles of your team, you can start to adapt to help them receive and understand your message. This can include mode of communicating (face-to-face or written), systematic versus direct (laying out a structure versus being short and to the point), formality preference, and even length of communication.

You may be asking, "With all the people on my team, how do I do an adapted communication for each person?" With a combined approach, you can quickly share information without creating a separate strategy for each team member.

If you have team members who are direct and prefer face-to-face, you can schedule a ten-minute virtual call that is transcribed for them to have later for their reference. If you have team members who have a more reserved style and like to process information, send out an email. Be sure to include a bullet point summary of takeaways and a bit of further qualification of the process, so each team member can go to the communication section they prefer first. And always, as a final step, confirm mutual understanding by asking clarifying questions and summarizing key action items. Keep in mind the personality of the team member and adjust your communication accordingly, without having to create a completely new strategy system.

The four DiSC types (D, i, S, C) each have a preferred communication approach. For a D-type personality, be specific, brief, and gone. For an i-type personality, be friendly, positive, and sociable. For an S-type personality, be empathetic, authentic, and patient. For a C-type personality, be prompt, prepared, and precise.

We all bring different preferences and tendencies to the workplace. Some of us focus on making rapid progress while others advocate for a more cautious approach. Some people seek out collaboration and interaction, while others prefer to go it alone.

The next two stories are about two specific DiSC types. There may be parts of both that resonate with you, as leaders tend to overlap and bring in different personality types into their leadership. The stories are meant to highlight gaps in communication when we are not in tune with who we are and who our audience is.

How Knowing Your Communication Style Can Be Life-Changing

John was a successful executive. His career was a textbook story of grit, ambition, and climbing the corporate ladder. He was known for his decisiveness, sharp intellect, and ability to deliver results under pressure. But behind the closed doors of his corner office, John often felt isolated. Meetings were transactional, feedback was scarce, and his personal life . . . well, that had unraveled years ago.

When his company announced a leadership workshop based on DiSC and emotional intelligence, John was skeptical. He wasn't "broken," he thought. "What value could understanding personality traits bring to someone with his track record?" Yet, the CEO was insistent, and John reluctantly signed up.

During the workshop, John learned that he had a D-style personality—dominant, driven, and laser-focused on results. While these traits had fueled his professional success, they had also come with blind spots. He tended to bulldoze through conversations, dismiss emotions, and prioritize outcomes over relationships. For the first time, John saw his behavior reflected back at him like a mirror.

One exercise required participants to reflect on how their communication style affected those around them. As John listened to stories from colleagues about how D-styles could be perceived—intimidating, impatient, or even cold—he felt a pang of recognition.

Then came a pivotal moment. The facilitator asked everyone to imagine how their personality and communication style might affect the people closest to them outside of work.

John froze. Memories came rushing back:

- The countless times he'd dismissed his wife's concerns with "Just handle it."
- The way his son stopped sharing stories from school because John would only critique his performance.
- The night his wife said she felt invisible in their marriage— and how he responded by telling her to "be less emotional."

By the end of the session, John wasn't just reflecting on his past; he was grieving it. He realized that his inability to adapt, to slow down, and to listen had cost him more than he ever imagined.

In a follow-up coaching session, John confided in the facilitator: "If I had learned this ten years ago, my life would look so different. I might still be married. My son might actually pick up the phone when I call."

From that day forward, John committed to change, not just for the sake of his team, but for himself. He began asking open-ended questions in meetings, pausing to ensure everyone had a voice. At home, he started sending his son simple text messages: "Proud of you." It was awkward at first, but over time, their conversations grew more frequent and meaningful.

John knew he couldn't rewrite the past, but the workshop gave him something equally powerful: the tools to shape a better future.

The Lunch Dilemma: An *S* Learns About Their Style

Angela sat in the leadership workshop nodding along as the facilitator described the different DiSC styles. She had taken the assessment earlier that week, and now, as the results were unpacked, she realized something—she was an *S* through and through. Steady, supportive, accommodating, and—if she was honest—sometimes a little too deferential.

As the session continued, the facilitator chuckled. "Now, let me give you a classic example of an *S* in action. Imagine two *S*'s trying to decide where to go for lunch."

The room erupted in laughter, but Angela wasn't quite sure why.

"They'll start with, 'Where would you like to go?'" the facilitator continued.

Angela smirked. That sounded familiar.

"The other *S* will immediately respond, 'Oh, I don't care—where would you like to go?'"

Angela laughed louder this time, glancing at Lisa, her coworker sitting next to her. They had literally had this conversation yesterday.

"And it will go on and on," the facilitator said, mimicking the back-and-forth. "'Oh, really, I'm good with anything.' 'No, no, whatever you want is fine!' Until, finally, someone—probably a *D* or an *I*—gets frustrated and just picks a place."

The room howled. Angela did, too, recognizing herself in the example. She could almost hear her more assertive colleagues groaning in exasperation.

As the laughter died down, the facilitator smiled. "Here's the thing—*S*'s are incredible team players. You value harmony, you're great listeners, and you genuinely care about making sure everyone is comfortable and happy. But sometimes, your go-with-the-flow nature can make decision-making tough for you and others."

Angela nodded. That was true. She hated the idea of imposing her preferences on others, but she also realized that her hesitancy might be more frustrating than helpful.

"So, here's your challenge," the facilitator continued. "Next time someone asks you where you want to go to lunch, just pick somewhere, or be very clear you want them to choose. It doesn't have to be the perfect choice if you choose."

Angela laughed again, but she also took the advice to heart. Maybe, just maybe, she'd suggest that new Italian place today instead of waiting for someone else to decide.

Actions To Take

Establish A Baseline For Your Communication

Ensure you have a baseline of your current communication skills. You can use any personality assessment, and I recommend Everything DiSC. Study your profile so that you understand your own preferences, motivators, and stressors and understand how that impacts others styles.

Get To Know Your Team

Ideally, have your team take the assessment(s) also. Once everyone has taken this, you will have a common language to use, and communication becomes easier and more effective. Knowing each team member will help to avoid misunderstandings and support each person's communication style.

Don't Stop Learning

Lastly, continue to apply what you have learned and continue to learn, and use the online learning system so that you can adapt as your team learns new skills and becomes more proficient in their communication style and how they communicate across the team.

4

Develop Emotional Intelligence

When dealing with people, remember you are not dealing with creatures of logic, but with creatures of emotion.
DALE CARNEGIE

The definition of emotional intelligence (EQ) is the agility to read the emotional and interpersonal needs of a situation and respond accordingly. Agility is the key word—how quickly can you assess and respond to the situation?

A comprehensive study by Six Seconds revealed that overall EQ, particularly skills like optimism, self-regulation, and empathy, has dropped globally.[15] The pandemic heightened stress, leading to decreased creativity and compassion, which are crucial components of emotional intelligence.

Younger generations have experienced the most significant drops in emotional intelligence. A study showed a decline in emotional intelligence on a global scale from 2019 to 2023.[16] Gen Z in particular seems to be up against an emotional crisis, with over 50 percent scoring a low workplace satisfaction score, thus suggesting an increased risk of experiencing burnout.

The Impact Of Technology And Social Media

A meta-analysis published in the *Journal of Personality* found that increased access to technology and social media is associated with lower levels of well-being and self-control.[17] The study, which analyzed data from seventy studies conducted between 2001 and 2019, suggested that online interactions might be replacing in-person communication, thereby reducing opportunities for emotional closeness and empathy.[18]

These statistics underscore the challenges posed by recent global events and technological advancements, highlighting the need for targeted interventions to rebuild and enhance emotional intelligence across all age groups, particularly in the workplace. Put another way, the workforce is losing emotional intelligence, which can affect performance, conflict resolution, and organizational resilience.

The assessment and training provided in the Everything DiSC Agile EQ model (shown on the next page) is a great way to get a baseline and create a development plan for becoming more agile as a leader.

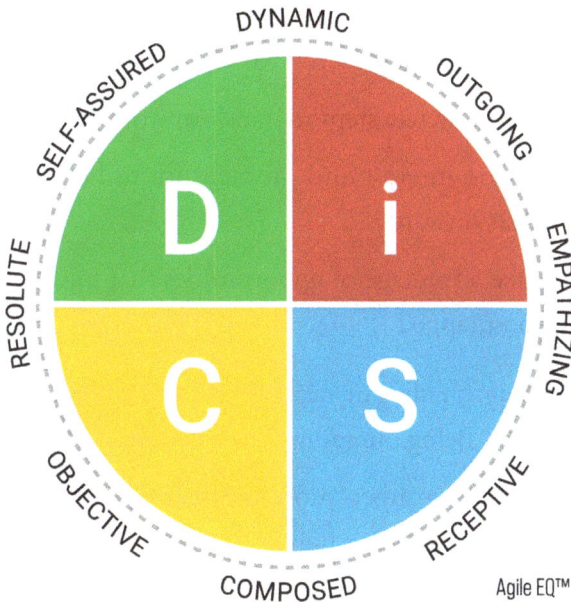

Agile EQ™

Mindsets Defined

Below are the different mindsets in the model and how to leverage them in your daily life as a leader. Each one is critical in the further development of emotional intelligence and being able to grow as an effective leader:

- Self-assured: projecting confidence and taking charge. Being self-assured allows you to:
  - Convey to others your conviction in your opinions and ideas
  - Ensure that others take what you say seriously and treat your ideas and rights with respect
  - Inspire confidence in your ideas and abilities

- Dynamic: influencing others and taking action on new ideas. Being dynamic allows you to:
  - Take concrete steps to transform your ideas into reality
  - Create interest and momentum to help move your ideas forward
  - Take advantage of opportunities that might otherwise go untapped

- Outgoing: building up relationships and expressing unfiltered thoughts. Being outgoing allows you to:
  - Create stronger, more rewarding relationships and reinforce existing bonds
  - Build trust by encouraging open, honest interactions
  - Develop a network of allies you can draw on for support as you work toward your goals

- Empathizing: understanding others and reaching out to be supportive. Being empathetic allows you to:
  - Anticipate how your actions or decisions might affect others
  - Support a coworker who is struggling
  - Gain deeper knowledge of another person

- Receptive: keeping an open mind and considering other perspectives. Being receptive allows you to:
  - Collaborate in a healthy and respectful way
  - Seek out the strongest solution when multiple ideas are on the table

- Balance the needs of multiple parties

- Composed: remaining calm and diplomatic. Being composed allows you to:
    - Avoid rash choices in the heat of the moment
    - Allow yourself or others space for careful thought and consideration
    - De-escalate tension

- Objective: thinking rationally and clearly. Being objective allows you to:
    - Distance yourself from your own biases
    - Gain insight into a subject that creates strong emotions in others
    - Identify the critical facts in a complicated or confusing situation

- Resolute: resisting pressure to cave in. Being resolute allows you to:
    - Defend your ideas
    - Stand up to strong personalities
    - Resist the influence of others

When I conduct training on improved communication and emotional intelligence, one of the tips I give that people remember comes from military usage. These questions may be familiar:

- What information do I have?

- Who needs to know it?

- Have I told them? And, to add to what we have learned from DiSC and Agile, have I communicated it in a way that they heard and understood?

It is remarkable how focusing on these three questions streamlines communication in organizations. These questions seem simple, and in their simplicity, there is a direct path forward to being adaptable.

With the rise of digital and remote work, there are now new barriers to developing and demonstrating emotional intelligence. Most leaders recognize how emotional intelligence affects an inclusive and collaborative work environment. In addition, the link between emotional intelligence, mental health, and stress management is receiving more attention.

Resilient leaders will need to continue to adapt their skill set to ongoing virtual interactions and online communications. Here is a story that shows the importance of understanding the nuances of virtual interactions.

Changing Communications For The Online World

When the world shifted to remote work, Stephanie, a senior manager at a tech company, prided herself on her ability to maintain productivity within her team. She scheduled weekly check-ins, created detailed project timelines, and ensured that deadlines were met. On paper, everything looked fine. But behind the screens, things weren't going as smoothly as she thought.

During one of our coaching sessions, Stephanie admitted to feeling frustrated. "I'm doing everything I did when we worked in the office, but people seem disengaged. I don't know how to fix it," she said, exasperated.

I asked her to describe a recent team meeting. "Well, I go through the agenda, check in on progress, and assign next steps," she explained.

"And what happens after that?" I asked.

"They don't really say much. Cameras are mostly off. It feels like I'm talking into a void."

That last sentence stopped me. "Talking into a void" was a perfect way to describe how many leaders felt in the early days of virtual work. But the truth was, Stephanie hadn't adapted her leadership style to this new environment. What worked in person—reading the room, catching subtle nonverbal cues, or having a quick chat at someone's desk—didn't translate to Zoom, Teams, or Google.

I asked her to consider how her meetings might appear from her team's perspective.

"When everyone's cameras are off, there's no accountability," she realized. "And when I stick to the agenda so rigidly, there's no room for connection."

We worked together to reframe her approach. First, she started opening meetings with personal check-ins, such as: "What's something good that's happened this week?" This small change gave her insight into how her team was really doing—and signaled that she cared about them as individuals, not just contributors.

Next, she shifted from rigid agendas to collaborative discussions. She used breakout rooms for brainstorming, asked for feedback on decisions in real time, and strongly encouraged cameras to be on, while respecting the occasional need for flexibility.

The results were almost immediate. "It's like night and day," she told me a month later. "People are more engaged, and I'm seeing ideas I didn't even know they had before."

Stephanie's story is a reminder that virtual leadership requires intentional adaptation. You can't rely on physical presence to create trust or connection. Instead, you need to lean into empathy, clarity, and creativity—meeting people where they are, even if they're behind a screen.

The ability to adapt isn't just a nice-to-have skill for virtual leaders; it's a necessity. Leaders who recognize this can transform their teams, fostering engagement and connection in ways that make the distance feel irrelevant.

Picking Up On New And Subtle Clues

In today's remote and hybrid work environments, leaders need to hone their skills and ability to pick up on more subtle clues during video and virtual interactions. Video calls present limited cues, unlike in-person meetings, where body language is more readily apparent. Leaders now need to pick up on voice inflections, changes in energy and engagement levels, and micro expressions. A team member who consistently keeps their camera off or seems distracted might be signaling disengagement or a deeper challenge they're facing.

Developing this awareness requires focused attention, emotional intelligence, and a willingness to address any underlying issues in a supportive manner.

It is also important for leaders to pay attention to the dynamics of group calls, just as we do for in-person dynamics. Are some voices dominating while others remain silent? Are there changes in frequency or quality of contribution from typically active members? Subtle shifts reveal team dynamics or individual concerns that need to be addressed.

Leaders need to create an environment that encourages participation by asking thoughtful, open-ended questions and giving quieter team members opportunities to share by applying other techniques like round-robin processes.

By sharpening our ability to read virtual cues, leaders can demonstrate empathy and strengthen relationships, even across screens. This attentiveness fosters trust and helps employees feel seen and valued, ultimately contributing to higher engagement, stronger collaboration, and better team performance and productivity.

Actions To Take

Understand Your Employees

This is something worth repeating: Understanding a baseline of where your employees are related to the mindsets will allow you to understand their strengths and areas that are outside their comfort zone. This is very different from "weaknesses," as these become targeted areas for improvement rather than having a negative connotation.

Keep In Mind The What, Who, And How

Consider the what, who, and how when looking at emotional intelligence and communication: What information do I actually have? Who needs to know this information? How have I shared this information? It is imperative to consider all of these questions.

Understand Your Decision Process

There is a saying that I have heard in the corporate world: Business decisions not based on business results lead to disaster. Are you basing your decision on business or emotions? When you make your next business decision, stop for a second and ask yourself, "What business information or model is the decision predicated on?"

5

Run More Effective Meetings

Good fortune is what happens when opportunity meets with planning.
THOMAS EDISON

I t has been said that for most workers, the only thing they hate more than meetings is the work the meetings get them out of. Even in the *Harry Potter* movie franchise, Hagrid talked about how they started the meeting with each person going around and saying why they were there. In short, workers find meetings to be a time suck, with nothing actually accomplished in the meeting, other than planning for the next meeting.

The issue of effective meetings has been exacerbated in recent years with virtual meetings (forcing people to join from anywhere), including the following:

- **Increased meeting load:** HR Dive reported that since the pandemic began, the number of meetings per person has increased by 13 percent.[19] Even with the total time spent in meetings going down, there is still a sense of overload and reduced overall productivity.

- **Meeting fatigue:** The phenomenon of "Zoom fatigue" has become widespread, with many employees reporting feeling drained after a day of virtual meetings. A survey by global staffing firm Robert Half and summarized by HR Executive found that 76 percent of employees experience frequent meeting fatigue, and 38 percent of remote workers believe that excessive meetings prevent them from getting their work done.[20]

- **Decline in meeting quality:** A study by MIT Sloan Management Review discovered that only 50 percent of meetings are effective.[21] This perceived meeting quality declines when reviewing virtual meetings, as many lack the engagement and spontaneity of in-person interactions. Harvard Business Review conducted a further study where 68 percent of employees reported not having enough uninterrupted focus time during the workday.[22] And that research indicated that up to one-third of meetings were unnecessary.

- **Technical issues and distractions:** Virtual meetings are often plagued by technical issues, such as poor internet connectivity, audio problems, and software glitches. Additionally, remote work environments can introduce distractions that are less prevalent in traditional office settings, further reducing meeting effectiveness.

Facilitator training has been our flagship training course with hundreds of participants from CEOs and executives to first-level supervisors. The need for better meeting practices exists now more than ever. There is an art and science to running effective meetings, and there are tools that leaders can learn and apply. There are several items that should be standard practices, such as setting clear agendas, limiting the number of participants, ensuring meetings are necessary, and leveraging collaboration tools effectively.

If you are ready to up your meeting game, using the Cycle of Facilitation will get you there.

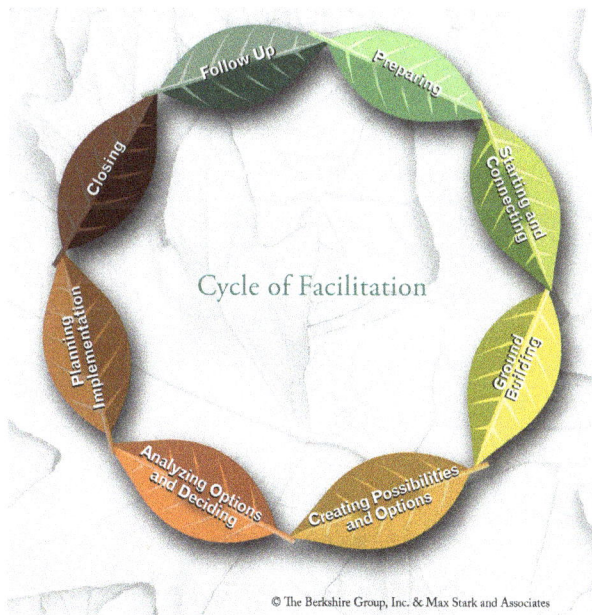

Cycle of Facilitation

© The Berkshire Group, Inc. & Max Stark and Associates

Rather than looking at this as making a meeting effective, reframe it as successful group work. That is exactly what your meetings should be: group work to move toward a common goal.

Developing Key Facilitator Skills

As the leader, you will become the facilitator of the meetings, and you need several skills to ensure that group meetings run efficiently and produce results. With learning facilitation comes new skills that you will need to hone to keep a sustained, high-involvement environment.

Skill Number One: Maintaining Awareness And Objectivity

Effective facilitators are skilled in stepping back from a meeting and keeping the big picture in mind. This will help you monitor the facilitation process. As a facilitator, this is not the time to champion your own ideas. Rather, the task at hand is to encourage the participation of the rest of the group.

This can be particularly challenging when, as a leader-facilitator, you have a stake in the work and the outcome. As a positional facilitator, you may have an opinion and wish to step in to share it with the group. If you will be actively participating in the discussion, articulate clearly that you are stepping out of the facilitator role to avoid alienating the group and to be clear about what your role is at all times.

Skill Number Two: Designing The Process/Meeting

It is imperative to organize the meeting and design the process for dealing with the content in advance. This includes documenting goals for the meeting, deciding who will be participating and their individual roles in the meeting, outlining an agenda, sharing what information may be needed by participants in advance, and determining how you will record the meeting. Designing the process for dealing with the content for instance, will it be open discussion, flowcharting, small group work, or other methods eliminates wasted time and keeps the meeting on track.

Skill Number Three: Building A Supportive Environment

Everyone who has been chosen to participate adds value to the meeting and should have a voice, regardless of whether they are more introverted.

An effective facilitator encourages participation from the entire group by using techniques that make everyone feel comfortable and engaged. These techniques include asking open-ended questions, protecting proposals even if they are incomplete or just a rough draft, showing empathy, and recognizing and reinforcing constructive engagement in the meeting.

Skill Number 4: Listening And Paraphrasing

Truly paying attention to what is being said can be challenging. Our minds tend to formulate responses to comments, and we lose our ability to track what someone else is sharing. With good eye contact and nonverbal cues such as nodding, a facilitator can encourage both listening and participation.

Paraphrasing can also help all team members to fully hear and understand what has just been said. This is a technique of stating back to the individual what you heard them say. Restate main points and resist using the same exact words. You may respond by saying, "What I heard you say was . . .." This is a skill that must be practiced over time. It is not critical to get the paraphrasing perfect—the speaker will correct if you missed something.

Listening and paraphrasing are invaluable tools because they dramatically improve communication, not only for the speaker and facilitator but for the entire group. It demonstrates listening and respect for the speaker by valuing what the speaker has to say. This, in turn, encourages the speaker to be more inclined to listen and respect other speakers during the meeting.

Skill Number 5: Visualizing The Discussion

In this final skill, the facilitator captures major points in writing so the entire group can see them. To maintain focus and develop ideas during the meeting, the facilitator should write down points as they are being made. This can be done using a flip chart, whiteboard, computer with a projector, or other similar tools, in person or, for remote or hybrid meetings, using one of the many tools included in electronic meeting software.

The written points should be legible and in a location where the whole group can see them. Again, by maintaining objectivity and listening, you will be able to capture the speaker's point, not what you think it should be. When writing, continue the conversation with the group versus saying what you are writing.

By leveraging and refining these skills, you can create a meeting environment that encourages the entire group to participate fully and share their opinions, perspectives, and expertise.

How A Commitment To Good Facilitation Can Stop A Train Wreck

Facilitating strategic planning sessions had always been rewarding, but it came with its challenges. This time, I had been brought in to guide a nonprofit board through aligning their vision for the future. The organization had a passionate team of leaders, and while passion is an asset, it can also spark conflict.

After our second session, the board chair approached me with a request: "Would you sit in on our next board meeting? I'd love your perspective on how we handle things on a regular basis." I was intrigued as I had picked up on some dynamics during the planning sessions that I wanted to confirm.

I agreed, curious to observe the dynamics of the group during their regular interactions. What I wasn't prepared for was just how volatile the meeting would become.

About thirty minutes into the discussion, tensions began to rise—the topic was a significant budget allocation that had divided the room into opposing camps. The chair was trying to guide the conversation, but the tone quickly escalated. Two board members—both standing now—were yelling across the table at each other, their voices bouncing off the walls.

I wasn't sure if this was par for the course or an anomaly, so I gave it a moment, thinking perhaps the chair had a plan to bring it under control. But as the shouting continued and the group fractured into side conversations, the chair glanced at me, her eyes filled with equal parts frustration and helplessness. She leaned slightly in my direction and said, "Can you help?"

Taking a deep breath, I stood and addressed the group. "Let's pause for a moment," I said, my voice firm, raised a bit to be heard, but calm. The room quieted, though the tension was palpable. I guided them through a simple process to de-escalate emotions:

everyone took turns sharing their perspective, uninterrupted, while the others practiced active listening. It wasn't an instant fix, but by the end of the exercise, the tone of the conversation had shifted from combative to collaborative, and they had a process to make a decision.

After the meeting, the chair and I sat down to debrief. She shook her head and sighed. "I didn't know what to do," she admitted. "I need to develop better skills to handle situations like this."

Her honesty was refreshing. It takes humility to admit you need help. We discussed strategies for developing the agenda, accounting for both process and content, as well as managing group dynamics, including setting clear expectations for behavior. Additionally, we explored how to assert authority as a facilitator without stifling open dialogue. Over time, I worked with her to strengthen her facilitation skills, giving her tools to guide productive conversations—even in the face of conflict.

Reflecting on that experience, I realized how common it is for leaders, even highly capable ones, to struggle with facilitation, especially managing conflict. Many board chairs or team leaders are chosen for their expertise, passion, or seniority, not necessarily for their ability to navigate complex group dynamics. But with the right tools and training, anyone can learn to facilitate meetings that move from chaos to clarity.

Stages For Group Collaboration And Work

Getting full participation in a group meeting is the start of effectiveness. Now it is time to move that group to better collaboration.

There are several stages that will help you facilitate and allow group collaboration in your organization. And it begins with preparation.

Preparing

In this step, it is essential to get down to basics. For example, is a meeting necessary, or would an email suffice? Who are the most important players to be present at this meeting? Will other individuals enhance the meeting or potentially derail it? Will this meeting be held virtually or in person?

Understanding these elements will lay the foundation for the next step.

Starting And Connecting

How many times have you seen participants come in just at the start of the meeting, or a few minutes after, and be unprepared or distracted? When planning your agenda, be sure to allocate a few minutes to ground the meeting. This allows people to become mentally prepared for the work ahead (because meetings should be about action). Provide a structured way for them to connect to each other and the topic at hand, so the meeting can produce desired results.

Ground Building

Providing context around the situation and ensuring a clear understanding is the next critical step. This is not where you create a plan. This step is to build awareness of factors in play. Participants may want to move right into problem-solving. It is the leader's responsibility to guide them back to this step; otherwise, you may have people trying to solve different problems.

Creating Possibilities And Outcomes

In this stage, the group creates possible approaches. This is where creativity and extraordinary thinking come into play. By supporting diverse and nonlinear thinking, the group can start to think outside the triangle. This also allows a fresh perspective to come in to create a transformative approach to the problem at hand. Resist the participants' urge to simply pick the solution that has "always worked."

Analyzing Options And Deciding

What are the merits of each alternative, and what are the pros and cons of each approach? By reviewing each possible approach and comparing them, the group can reach an agreement on the best choice and ensure that each contributor feels heard. This is where rational judgment, including historical data and individual experiences, can come into play to help with the final decision.

Planning The Implementation

You have made the decision on the best course of action. Great! Now comes pulling the trigger. How will you put this plan into action? What resources are necessary? Who are the best people to get this implementation across the finish line? What are the steps and schedule? By laying out a systematic approach, including order of steps and a timeline, the group has a clear understanding of the implementation and their role in the successful outcome.

Each step is critical to move the group through a defined process and work toward more effective meetings and interactions. Participants will become familiar with the process, and the step flow will become more natural. That will, in turn, create meetings with purpose and happier participants.

Actions To Take

Understand Process Versus Content
Differentiate process from content when planning meetings. Are you looking at the process for each section of the meeting content? How will you cover each topic, for example: open discussion, small groups and then large, round robin brainstorming?

Ensure Adequate Prep Time
You need to build in time for preparation. If you show up to the meeting unprepared, without an agenda or an understanding of what you hope the outcome of the meeting will be, you are wasting everyone's time. Plan out the agenda, including process, content, timing, and outcomes for each component, and ideally share it with participants in advance.

Engage Meeting Participants
Effective leaders understand how to engage each person in the meeting to ensure full participation and maximum impact. Each person was invited for a specific purpose. What is the purpose for each person, and how do they move the project and deliverables forward? Is there information that you can and should provide in advance to get the most out of each participant?

Follow The Process

Always follow the process you have created so each meeting has a planned and clear structure. When it is evident what the process is for the meeting, all participants can come prepared, as they know what the flow will be.

Learn Adaptive Decision-Making

It's become apparent that you can't take forever to make decisions in today's world. Things are moving way too rapidly. By the same token, having a process that you use to be situationally aware and to make decisions that are not totally off the cuff is a good model. After all, decisions made without data can be catastrophic for your organization.

This decision-making model is to read, assess, decide, and act, or RADA.

The Dogfights Of The Korean War

During the Korean War, US fighter pilots flying the F-86 Sabre were often up against the superior performance of the Soviet MiG-15. On paper, the MiG-15 was faster, more agile, and better armed. Yet, American pilots maintained a significantly higher kill ratio (estimated at 10:1 in favor of the F-86). Why was that?

This success was largely due to the way US pilots executed decision-making under pressure, using what can be understood as the RADA framework:

1. **Read (observe):** Pilots constantly scanned their environment, looking for subtle shifts in enemy behavior, aircraft movements, and changes in the tactical situation.

2. **Assess (orient):** They interpreted the information rapidly, factoring in altitude, position, and the enemy's likely intentions. This ability was enhanced by the F-86's bubble canopy and better hydraulics, giving pilots superior visibility and maneuverability.

3. **Decide:** Based on the assessment, pilots quickly chose their course of action—whether to evade, engage, or reposition for a tactical advantage.

4. **Act:** They executed their decisions swiftly and decisively, often outmaneuvering MiG pilots, who were slower to adapt due to rigid Soviet command structures and less flexibility in the cockpit.

The agility and adaptability of American pilots—mirroring the RADA model—allowed them to make better decisions faster than their adversaries, even when faced with a technically superior aircraft.

This story exemplifies how leaders (or pilots) can succeed by rapidly reading the environment, assessing variables, making decisions, and acting decisively, even in high-stakes situations.

Let's break down the RADA model in more detail for you as the leader.

Starting With The Read

When you read the situation, you gather as much data as you can. This means continuing to gather data for the duration of time that you have to make the decision. This could be three minutes or three days, and information gathering is a key objective.

In today's world, for leaders who tend to be a little bit more methodical, this step has to be quicker than it has been in the past. However, data can also be gathered at a faster rate in our digital world. And with data capture, recognizing the issue or opportunity can be faster and more accurate.

This step also provides context for the situation. No decision is ever made in a vacuum, and having context for an issue allows for better understanding.

There are many leaders who want to spend more time gathering data and get stuck in this step. Learning to make decisions quicker is not only important, but has become a necessary skill.

Utilizing this model and ingraining in your mind the steps of this process will provide you with the formula to make these decisions quicker while still gathering necessary data. This will allow you to read the situation and move to the assessment phase, which centers around people, processes, and technology. Then you will be able to decide what to do and either act on it yourself or involve the appropriate people to take action.

Time To Assess

Imagine as a leader, you are doing this process. You cannot gather a hundred percent of the information you need. By the same token, you cannot use just 10 percent of the information. What percentage of the information do you look for when you have to pull the trigger and make a decision?

On average, leaders get between 70 and 90 percent of the data they need. There are times when you will have more, but that is going to be the rarity. This is where your intuition comes in. You have to read and assess, but things also have to align from an authenticity perspective as a leader when you make that decision.

At this stage, leaders also break down the situation to understand the various components and how those components work (or don't work) together. This also helps to explore any underlying causes, potential outcome scenarios, and any risks that come with each potential outcome.

Next, You Must Decide

After you have made your assessments and confirmed information and feelings, it is time to choose. Sometimes those decisions are easy, and other times they are hard. As Ruth Chang states in her 2014 TED Talk, hard choices are precious opportunities—they are not a curse but a godsend.[23] They are positive because the choices that you make are a reflection of who you are and who your organization is. Once you have all the information that you are gathering, which choice best aligns with who you are or want to be as a leader and with the values and mission of the organization?

In the decision phase, it is critical to consider the feasibility of a choice, how that is aligned with overall business goals, and what the potential impact of that decision is. With the decision, are there any unforeseen setbacks or new problems that will arise?

A scenario that comes to mind is in *Star Wars: Episode IV—A New Hope*. Luke Skywalker has rescued Princess Leia, only to be chased by Stormtroopers.[24] They take a wrong turn and end up at a drop-off. Luke closes the door behind them and, because he cannot find the lock, blasts the controls to keep the door closed. It is only then that he realizes he also has prevented them from extending the bridge across the drop-off to escape. In the moment, the feasibility of the choice was clear and aligned with the goal of not getting caught or killed. The impact of the decision, however, created a new problem that had to be overcome.

Finally, You Will Act

After you have made the decision, it is time to act. As leaders, that generally means that you are sharing your decision with others in some way—that you are looking for them to "buy in" to your decision. How you communicate your decision will affect how successful the implementation of it is.

The implementation of the decision is only the starting point. The decision needs to be monitored and potentially adjusted as new information comes to light.

This process allows for a tested and effective way to make decisions quickly and under pressure. After all, isn't that the norm you are now seeing?

Embracing The Hard Choice

In her TED Talk, Ruth Chang also discussed that hard choices are a godsend because they help us to become the distinct people that we are. These hard choices seem like they cause agony, but they actually uncover a hidden power that each of us, including leaders, possesses.

Hard choices are challenging because of the way the alternatives relate to one another. Neither appears better than the other overall. In addition, there are hard choices that are smaller that we still make every day. Her example is when you choose to eat the healthy bran cereal over the doughnut.

There is a misconception among leaders as well. Struggling with hard choices does not make leaders less effective or less intelligent. If leaders do struggle, there may be a desire to choose the "safest" choice. However, that introduces the idea that one choice truly is better than the other. The fact of the matter is that hard choices are hard because there is no best option, and, at the same time, they are also not equally good.

When faced with a difficult decision, we often assume that if just one factor in one of the options improved, the choice would become easier. But in many cases, it wouldn't. That's because we tend to treat each option as if its value can be clearly measured and compared—better, worse, or equal.

But what if there's another way to relate options?

Consider the idea of options being "on a par"—not better or worse, but in the same league of value while differing in kind. This introduces a compelling shift: we aren't just choosing between predefined values; we have the power to shape the scenario so that one option becomes the right choice *for us*.

This is the distinction between following logic and creating reasons, between relying on external validation and trusting our internal compass.

Drifters allow the world to write their story and determine the choices they make. Leaders can apply their own agency behind the hard decision and remove morality (right versus wrong). This allows leaders to express the distinct individuals they are and view hard choices as the power to create the future they move into.

Actions To Take

Practice Scenario Thinking

Regularly explore what-if scenarios to anticipate potential outcomes and identify creative solutions. This helps leaders build mental agility and stay flexible in the face of uncertainty.

Seek Diverse Perspectives

Engage with team members, peers, or mentors who bring different experiences, viewpoints, and problem-solving approaches. Diverse input sharpens decision-making and reduces blind spots.

Embrace Experimentation

Start small-scale experiments to test new ideas or strategies before committing to large-scale implementation. This builds adaptability by encouraging a mindset of learning, iteration, and refinement.

7

Foster Group
Problem-Solving

Alone we can do so little; together we can do so much.
HELEN KELLER

You may not believe it, but problem-solving is actually a journey. As a leader, you guide your team to facilitate change and achieve new successes, all with minimal involvement from you. And each team member can step into the role of leader when it is appropriate during the process.

It all starts with a mindset. Continuous improvement may no longer be as trendy. But as leaders, we should be continuously improving and be interested in creating mental resilience in our organizations and our people. When you bring people together for meetings that are being run to get the most out of the meetings and the participants, you begin to foster a resilient attitude.

Why bring people into a room if you are going to talk about an issue and not actually have participants add value and work together to solve that problem? The people who work for you are the people who ideally have the expertise in areas that you do not. And wins build up an individual's mental resilience.

As a leader, you are not the all-answer person. You need to have a process to get to the root causes. Otherwise, you're putting Band-Aids on things. If you don't get to the root cause, you're going to be right back in the same spot in six months, solving the exact same problem.

Understanding that you are not the all-answer person will help your team to step up and address the problem. That, in turn, builds mental resilience if the solution is not readily present.

Just like in the movie *Jumanji*, individual skill sets may not be powerful on their own, but together, they can build a framework for continuous improvement and true gains in problem-solving, allowing success to manifest.

We invite you on a journey to problem-solving using a proprietary process we have developed. This process provides the roadmap that you and your team will use over and over. It is called continuous improvement, not one-time improvement. This journey for problem-solving is a formula and happens in six distinct phases.

Phase I: Define And Organize

There may be several problems on the table. Determining which problem is the one to tackle now can feel daunting. The easiest way to determine which opportunity to work on ties into the strategic significance of the potential improvement. By looking at data to determine the impact of solving a problem, you can choose based on objectivity.

Handling one problem at a time also focuses resources on the specific issue to be solved and ensures it is resolved completely. One of those resources will be the team members pulled together who are best equipped to solve the problem.

Where are you bringing together the appropriate group of people, and how are you organizing them around the problem? With this team, how are you setting them up for success? Do you have a plan in place to determine the desired outcome, how it aligns with bigger strategic goals, and how performance will be measured? Team members also should have some skin in the game and want to see the desired outcome.

Through group problem-solving, you, as the leader, also help the group identify strategically significant opportunities. Most of your employees will already have a good understanding of the issues. By facilitating group problem-solving, the result is a high degree of ownership by employees. This is especially significant if the organization lacks a formal strategic plan or has limited employee buy-in.

But be aware that it is possible to work on an issue that is not necessarily of strategic importance. For example, there could be consensus to improve the website design, but investing in an e-commerce platform for customers to take ownership of the buying process would have a greater impact.

Phase II: Understand The Current State

How well do you understand the current process? Do you have enough to modify or even break it? Documenting the current process using a flowchart provides common ground and a reference point for all team members. Part of this flowchart involves identifying both customers and suppliers.

Your processes do not exist within a vacuum. They are there to meet the needs of your customers. Who are those customers (both internal and external), and who are the suppliers that support the process? Within those processes are also key performance measures (KPMs), helping you determine what part of the process satisfies the customer experience, and what part does not. By collecting data and reviewing the KPMs, you will have a full picture of the current state.

This is also a great opportunity to document what is working well ("prouds") and what is not ("sorries"). This can include areas such as financial performance, reputation, teamwork, communication, implementation, general leadership, business acumen, customer service, processes, and technology.

Phase III: Search For Root Causes

Initially, this requires some free thinking and brainstorming. What are all the possible causes for the problem? There are no wrong answers here or wrong ideas. Write down all possible causes, no matter how unconventional.

When you have documented all possible causes, it is time to develop a cause-and-effect diagram. This tool accomplishes two primary tasks. First, it allows categories for the data and possible causes. Second, it allows you to ask "why" to each possible root cause, ensuring it is indeed a root cause and not just a symptom.

It provides needed drill-down thinking to test an idea and find the most fundamental effect. This also sets up the root-cause analysis, pulling in both data and group expertise to find a consensus of the root cause. Once you have identified the root cause, you can proceed to develop solutions.

As an example, a retailer sees a 15 percent drop in customer satisfaction over the last quarter. To identify potential causes, the retailer employs the Five Whys method, where for each answer, the question "why?" is repeatedly asked.

The retailer finds two potential causes: long checkout times and unhelpful staff.

Through the root-cause analysis, it was discovered that the long checkout times are due to an outdated point-of-sale system that takes longer to process and sometimes requires a reboot to continue the sale. For the unhelpful staff, a root-cause analysis shows that there is high turnover in the position and insufficient training of new staff with the products.

Both issues could potentially contribute to lower customer satisfaction when purchasing. And both have very different solutions that can be implemented. Furthermore, both problems are linked, so addressing both will have the biggest impact on customer satisfaction scores.

Phase IV: Develop Solutions

When we search for root causes, we might end up being tempted to fall back on tried-and-true solutions. Now is the time to think outside the box and stimulate new ideas for problem-solving. The first part of the process is merely to allow free thinking to come up with possible solutions.

Once you have documented a list of possibilities, you can now go through each one, again using data as well as the experience of the group, to uncover the best solution. This includes ensuring that you have not overlooked any potential obstacles or consequences of the solution. Reaching a consensus on the best solution can include evaluating the time, budget, and resources needed to implement. This is also the phase to outline what the next steps are for the solution.

In the above retail example, there may be a discussion about which solution should be launched first to achieve maximum impact. If training is redone and then a new point-of-sale system is introduced, training will have to be revisited yet again to train on the new system. While it may seem that training would be the first choice, it may be more prudent to update the old point-of-sale system and then incorporate this new system into a revamped training process.

Phase V: Develop And Present Recommendations

Rarely does a group tasked to develop a solution for a problem do so in an echo chamber. This phase is where a full recommendation is created and presented to those who were not part of the group but are key to the adoption of the solution. Using the data and methodology of the prior phases, you will be able to create an outline of background, supporting documentation, and business case for the solution.

This could include a cost/benefit analysis, a pros and cons list, and anything else that makes the leaders able to arrive at the same conclusion as your team. Include the part of your research that discounted other solutions and any root-cause analysis that helped you get to your recommendation.

In this phase, a review should be conducted to determine why it is necessary (the cost of doing nothing), why it should be done now (cost-benefit analysis and risk analysis), and why this is the best solution for the issue.

Phase VI: Implement And Monitor

Who will do what and by when? Someone needs to be the champion of the project and have the authority to assign tasks, request budget, and have an implementation plan in place to go from concept to reality.

A plan needs to be in place for any internal resistance. How can you help those individuals adopt the new solution? Can you include any resisters in the implementation to allow them to be part of the solution? How do you handle those on the outside who want to change the solution or implementation? Who are your allies that can be voices of reason?

No matter how strong the solution and the implementation plan, resistance can delay and derail success.

It is also vital to monitor the implementation and aftermath of the solution being put into place. Is there an opportunity for backsliding to the old way of thinking? How can you help the rest of the organization develop a new habit and adopt this new solution? And how can you empower the rest of the organization to move in a new direction?

With this journey, there will be breakdowns on the road. However, with this process in place, you are providing leadership and guidance through actionable steps that, when followed correctly, influence the degree to which problem-solving leads to solutions and change.

Here is an example of the power of group problem-solving. A manufacturing company had very high scrap and slow productivity. A cross-functional team of shop-floor workers went through this process. It proposed to management a total reorganization of the shop floor, which would require significant time and money to implement. They decided to do it, and the company got a multi-hundred-thousand-dollar return on that investment. Yes, there was a cost associated at the front end, but the financial and cultural impacts were significant.

Actions To Take

Cultivate Active Listening Skills

Practice truly hearing and understanding diverse perspectives by listening without interrupting or prejudging. Summarize and reflect on what team members share to ensure clarity and foster a collaborative environment where everyone feels valued.

Master Questioning Techniques

Develop the ability to ask open-ended and thought-provoking questions that guide the group toward creative solutions. For example, instead of asking, "What's the problem?" ask, "What opportunities can we uncover in this challenge?"

Encourage Structured Collaboration

Use a structured methodology that looks at the current state, root-cause analysis, or affinity mapping to keep discussions organized and focused. Ensure all voices are heard, manage dominant personalities, and help the group reach alignment on actionable next steps.

Build And Model Resilience

The more you do, the more you fail.
The more you fail, the more you learn.
The more you learn, the better you get.
JOHN C. MAXWELL, *LEADERSHIP GOLD*

All the skills we're discussing are designed to help you develop your resilience. If you become better at making adaptive decisions, navigating the people part of leadership, leading people in effective communication, raising your emotional intelligence, and developing the mindset where those habits are second nature to you, then you become more resilient as a leader.

Leaders need to change because the world has changed. The same old, same old doesn't work—and this is true now more than ever. Personal and professional development are critical to becoming a resilient leader in these challenging times. If you want your business to grow, you must grow yourself and your leaders.

> Personal and professional development are critical to becoming a resilient leader in these challenging times.

We are all under more stress right now in these trying times. It isn't that things weren't uncertain before. However, with digital transformation, we must become more resilient to changes and the accompanying stress than ever before.

Mental Resilience Is A Growth Mindset

Mental resilience has to be worked on every day. The fortitude that comes with resilience is actually moving your skills as a leader into a growth mindset, not only for yourself, but for your team as well.

Each resilience story is different, yet they tend to share common themes. With the following real-life examples, leaders can hopefully find common ground and inspiration to overcome problems and setbacks, emerging more confident and stronger.

What Resilient Leadership Means: Janis Shinkawa, DVM

When Janis thinks of what "resilient leadership" means, she considers her years of learning from good and bad experiences that have shaped how she operates in the world today.

Janis shared this insight, "My life's mission statement at the bold age of twelve was to 'always make a positive impact.' Back then, it meant being a good friend, daughter, granddaughter, niece, teammate, classmate, student, or newspaper carrier (my first job). Now at fifty-five, it means so much more!"

She has become very resilient with her leadership, mainly because of her experiences in "leading" at a young age. She grew up as a very shy child in Hawaii. The report cards to her parents stated, "Janis is so quiet and shy; she needs to learn to speak up." She was overlooked for the "advanced" classes since other kids were more outspoken.

In seventh-grade band, there was a precise moment that made her decide not to be overlooked anymore.

"I knew I could lead and conduct a team, so I did . . . literally. I picked up the baton that was sitting on the music stand at the front of the band room, as everyone wanted to play a song, although we were all musically off-key. I remember being a little scared and then thinking that I had nothing to be scared of. No one else was taking the 'risk' to get up and lead, so why should they get mad at me? So, I led, got through the song, and never looked back."

Since then, she has had multiple leadership roles (and training opportunities) throughout high school, college, her first career as a CPA, and now as a veterinarian. Each instance taught her how to be a better leader by studying what works and what doesn't work, and understanding the underlying reasons. Paying attention to how you lead and learning from others—listening to the sometimes harsh but necessary feedback—is what helps to evolve your leadership style. This creates resilience in your leadership while you gain confidence in yourself and learn to detach from outcomes.

Janis says, "Resilient leadership is having a calm and steady approach to matters while making others feel safe. It is knowing that everything will be OK since you know your hard work and valuable inputs will create what is best to happen and a sense of peace with less worry or control. The age at which you develop resilient leadership is not the focus. The focus is enjoying peace and calm while influencing others for the purpose of making a positive impact."

A Resilience Story: Shaina Zazzaro

Shaina Zazzaro created a multimillion-dollar food delivery service company, Effortlessly Healthy Meals. But the road to that success point was anything but a straight line. When she first started, she was able to grow rapidly to one hundred customers. However, her infrastructure and processes were not ready for that customer load, and her quality suffered. She dropped down to seven remaining customers. At that point, she could have given up.

But she knew she had a viable product and a strong market and took the "failure" of losing customers as a reset button for her business processes. She looked at the mistakes and corrected them. With this smaller failure, she was able to set up her business for much larger success.

The key element was being able to use failure as a seed for greater success and to pivot within that setback. Instead of panicking, she conducted a root-cause analysis and gained valuable information that strengthened her company even further. What's more, because of her resilience, she also gained the confidence to move through future challenges to her success.

In fact, in 2024, her company was recognized by the Greater Rochester Chamber of Commerce as one of the region's top 100 fastest-growing companies. The initial setback did not define her or her organization. Instead, it provided her with the knowledge to change course and ultimately helped to solidify the right processes to ensure a quality product, regardless of how much she grew.[25]

A Journey Of Resilience Together: Bevan Evans

Bevan's mother founded Evans Industries in the late 1970s. Except for a brief three-year stint working elsewhere, Evans has been Bevan's professional home. It was always understood that she would take over when her mother retired. That unofficial transition began in 2018, as her mother started to slow down, and Bevan stepped in to manage the day-to-day operations.

That period was her first real test of resilience at work. For her, resilience is less about relentless pursuit of goals—though success is always rewarding—and more about the lessons learned along the way, both personally and professionally. Since 2018, those lessons have been some of the most challenging yet transformative experiences of her life.

One of the most challenging moments occurred in late 2019, when their largest customer significantly reduced their stock levels. Weekly orders stopped completely for more than six months, and by the fifth month, the company was struggling to pay its bills. It was a dark time, and Bevan grappled with the prospect of closing the business her mother had spent her life building. Then COVID-19 hit. Evans Industries was deemed an essential business and managed to secure a Paycheck Protection Program

(PPP) loan—a lifeline that allowed them to weather the storm. With the emotional support of her family and the determination of her staff, they pulled through.

When Bevan officially took the reins, the company was in disarray. They lacked accountability and processes for tracking time standards, inventory, scrap, and quality control. The financials were unreliable, and they didn't fully understand costs. Over the past five years, Bevan has focused on turning the business around, building confidence to attract new and diverse customers.

This transformation has required both her and her staff to grow. For instance, the plant supervisor—an employee with more than twenty years of experience—initially resisted necessary changes. Through situational leadership, Bevan guided him to adjust his approach and embrace their shared goals. Similarly, she used emotional intelligence techniques with both her office manager and plant supervisor to help them understand each other's communication styles and to work more effectively as a team.

What Bevan has learned is that leadership is not about a one-size-fits-all approach. It's about adaptability and resilience—choosing the right strategy for the people and situation at hand. By applying these techniques, she has not only grown as a leader but also helped her staff develop their skills and confidence.

Looking back, Bevan is proud of what her team has accomplished together. Each challenge has strengthened her belief in the importance of resilience and adaptability. More importantly, it has prepared her to face the future with confidence, knowing that she has the tools—and the team—to meet whatever comes next.

Actions To Take

Focus On Health And Well-Being

Prioritize physical health through regular exercise, sleep, and proper nutrition, as well as mental health by setting boundaries, practicing stress-management techniques, and seeking professional support when needed. Resilient leaders are those who take care of themselves first to show up fully for others.

Strengthen Your Support Network

Build and nurture relationships with mentors, peers, and trusted colleagues. A strong support system provides encouragement, perspective, and solutions during difficult times.

Develop A Personal Reflection Practice

Take time daily or weekly to reflect on challenges and identify lessons learned. Journaling or mindfulness practices can help you process emotions, maintain perspective, and strengthen your ability to bounce back from setbacks.

PART III

The Road Ahead

This may seem like a never-ending assignment. You must be strategic, lead your team, and possess additional skill sets to keep the company and its employees operating at optimal levels. You now need to possess both business acumen and soft skills for the future. This is a lot to digest.

The road ahead may seem difficult and, at times, even dangerous. However, as stated in earlier chapters, this isn't just about your journey. This is about leading your team into the future, armed with the skills and tools to thrive, not survive. Because, like it or not, these new skills are no longer nice-to-have skills. They are must-have skills in this new world.

The future work on yourself and your team will pay off in dividends. You will not only be better prepared for the struggles and shifts that lie ahead, but your team and organization will also be ready. That is and always will be the end goal. And a team that has all the necessary tools makes an organization strong and profitable.

So, let's chat further about how you can help your team help you.

9

Develop Your Team
For What's Ahead

Individuals play the game, but teams beat the odds.
Navy SEAL saying

The first thing that comes to mind when I think about developing your team is determining whether you will have a team or a group. As a manager and leader, there are times when you're managing a group of people who don't actually work together.

Start At The Beginning

As a leader, the first thing to decide is whether I have a group that I can make a high-performing group of individuals, or do I have a group of people who need to work together, and I must develop a team?

High-performing teams are few and far between. You're not necessarily going to go through the work that it takes to have an overall high-performing team, but making that decision up front is critical.

Ask yourself: "What do I need to have? What do I want to have?" Developing the team to have all the components for success is a lot of work. If we start with the basics, it begins with you being very clear about your leadership style.

What can they expect from you? What do you expect from them? First and foremost is developing boundaries. What are the boundaries? What are the expectations? Each person's leadership style is unique, and you do yourself and your team a service if you're clear about that upfront. Clarity of expectations is probably one of the biggest things that comes into play when you're having performance issues. If you're clear on expectations, you're clear on boundaries.

The Compass Calibration

What are you doing to get to know these people? As stated earlier in the book, I recommend the Everything DiSC model. Utilizing this tool allows you to understand them better: their personalities, their priorities, their preferences, their motivators, and their stressors. With that information, you can now have a common language.

Another wonderful aspect of the Everything DiSC model is that it provides insight into how others prefer to be treated. This goes beyond the golden rule of treating people the way you want to be treated and goes to the platinum rule: treat others the way *they* want to be treated.

When I'm leading people, one of the first things I do is that assessment. I can then use language that's common to all of us. If I am asked to communicate differently, I don't take it personally. I know that I may need to change my tone of voice and communicate in a different way to be more effective.

This process enables you to set expectations, establish a baseline of people's personalities, understand their preferences, and know how they work, among other things. You can then conduct meetings to bring them together around a work product, where they collaborate and accomplish tasks together.

A Side Note On Managing Expectations

One item that has stayed constant, which is important to remember, is what I call the block-and-tackle method, named because this methodology focuses on executing fundamental and repeatable actions. Every single manager, director, and C-suite executive needs to know the company policies, documented processes, and systems that exist across the organization, and be aligned and adept in them.

When you, as the leader, understand and excel at the basics (the block and tackle), it removes guesswork and speculation from the equation when it comes to individual employee management and makes your life easier. It removes bias and allows both the manager and the employee to refer to the policy and procedures that all parties agreed to upon starting work.

Yes, there may be a need to change the policy, but that is a conversation for a different time (and a different procedure to have HR modify the company policy). Anyone who manages and leads must fully understand and implement the company policies as they are presented at this moment. If you are unclear, ask for clarification to be in alignment.

Any adjustments to your leadership approach must align with the company's existing policies. These strategies are meant to complement, not replace, those policies. Today's employees expect leaders to both follow established procedures and enhance productivity by creating a supportive, effective work environment. Always ensure your actions are consistent with corporate guidelines, and if anything is unclear, seek clarification to stay aligned. As a leader, if you get good at the block-and-tackle items or the science of leadership within your organization, you can focus your energy on the "softer" people side of leadership.

Transforming Culture, One Letter At A Time

When I was consulting with a mid-size organization of about a thousand employees, the company was struggling with communication and collaboration across teams. Leaders described a lack of alignment, employees were frustrated with unclear expectations, and cross-departmental projects often became battlegrounds of conflicting styles.

The CEO knew something needed to change and decided to implement DiSC across the organization, starting with the leadership team. The goal was ambitious: to create a shared language that would not only improve communication but also help them build a more cohesive and adaptable culture.

The transformation began in the leadership workshops. As leaders learned about their own DiSC profiles, lightbulbs started going off. They realized that the communication breakdowns weren't due to a lack of skill or intent but often stemmed from differences in style. A high-D leader realized their directive tone was intimidating to a high-S team member, who needed time to process decisions. A high-C manager who clashed with a high-i colleague suddenly understood why their meticulous focus on details felt stifling to someone who thrived on creativity and spontaneity.

From there, we rolled DiSC out to the entire organization, including during new employee onboarding. Everyone learned their profile and how it influenced their work, communication, and interactions. More importantly, they learned how to flex their styles to collaborate effectively.

What followed was nothing short of remarkable. DiSC quickly became a part of the organization's DNA. Teams began using it as a common language—neutral, constructive, and focused on growth. People would say things like, "Can you lower your *D* a little so we can explore more options?" or "I'll raise my *C* and dig deeper into the details." These phrases, which might have been insulting in the past, were now embraced as helpful feedback.

The impact on the culture was phenomenal. Leaders were more intentional about how they assigned projects, placing people in roles that aligned with their strengths. Employees felt seen and understood, and the collaborative tension that once derailed projects now fueled creativity.

One of the leaders summed it up best in a follow-up session: "Before, we'd take everything personally—'Why are they so difficult?' or 'Why don't they just get it?' But now, we just say, 'Oh, that's just their different style.' It's like we've all learned a new language, and it's made us so much more effective as a team."

By the time the initiative was fully implemented, the organization had become a case study in the power of self-awareness and adaptability. They didn't just have better meetings and smoother projects; they had a culture where people truly understood each other—and themselves.

This experience reinforced for me that tools like Everything DiSC aren't just about understanding personalities; they're about unlocking potential, improving trust, and creating a shared language that transforms how people work together.

Actions To Take

Review Your Organization's Policies And Procedures

Ensure that you have reviewed the most recent version of your policies and are proficient in the basics of employee relations, time and performance management, and the associated systems. If not, develop a plan to become adept at them.

Clarify One Expectation Today

Choose an expectation that may be unclear—whether about performance, communication, or decision-making—and make it explicit with your team. If you're unsure what to choose, consider any expectation that isn't being met. How clear are you in your communication about what needs to happen?

Adjust Your Communication Approach

Develop a table that lists the members of your team and their corresponding personality styles. Identify one team member and experiment with adapting your communication to better connect with them. What opened up with this action?

10

Creating A High-Performance Culture In Uncertain Times

The way I think about culture is that modern humans have radically changed the way that they work and the way that they live. Companies need to change the way they manage and lead to match the way that modern humans actually work and live. We're trying to re-craft culture in a way that really matches that. I think that 99% of companies are kind of stuck in the '90s when it comes to their culture.
BRIAN HALLIGAN, CEO OF HUBSPOT

I n the age of uncertainty, you can still create a high-performance culture.

I had the privilege of working with a CEO and executive group over a twenty-five-year period. It really highlighted for me that developing a culture is critical.

Every organization has a culture. The question is, will you create an intentional culture that is world-class and high-performing, so they win and win often?

Simon Sinek famously said, "Start with *why*."[26] The CEO and executive group must understand why an intentional culture can make or break an organization. That "why" embodies the culture that is created and has an impact on how good a company we become.

As the leader of the company, you must also believe that culture is vital. You want to have a culture that people want to work in, and having one positively affects you from a financial perspective.

Vision, Alignment, Execution

There has to be a vision of why we want to create this. Are we all on the same page with why? This vision doesn't happen overnight. It takes time to develop a culture.

If you could wave a magic wand and move into the future, what would it look like? What type of people would be working for your organization? How would you describe the culture? Having that vision makes you have a goal that can be articulated.

Next, align the executives with the vision. Creating a vision that leaders understand and buy into is critical. This includes defining the vision and the values that support that vision. If you are going to create a world-class, high-performing culture, every process and system has to align with those values. They can't just be on a sign hanging up on a wall.

When I say everything has to be aligned, I mean that your accounting principles, your HR principles, and your IT principles are all aligned. The leaders of the organization, including you, must understand how each department impacts the vision and alignment, as well as how to develop a culture that aligns with your vision and values.

For example, suppose employee autonomy is a core company value and your vision is to foster a culture where employees feel empowered and responsible. In that case, HR should not implement a policy that contradicts that, such as one that restricts autonomy unnecessarily. Doing so creates misalignment between your stated values and actual practices. When that happens, you risk disengagement and the lack of belief in any of the stated values.

To be in alignment also means *you* are fully committed to the vision and values. For example, are you willing to fire your high-performing salesperson because they behave in a way that is not in line with the company's values? If you can't say "yes, I am willing to fire that person, even though they're producing some significant revenue," then you are out of alignment. This person is too valuable to let go, and yet too painful to keep. If they are kept, the loud signal it sends to other employees is that the values aren't lived in the organization, and thus it undermines the culture.

If you claim these are your values, but someone is not behaving in a way that aligns with those values, then you risk making the entire organization out of alignment. And people will see that action before they read what's hanging on the wall. Once you know that you personally are in alignment, you can move to execution to establish the culture that is your North Star.

How do we develop leaders throughout the organization, from the first-level supervisor to the top, who will embody and own those values as if they owned the company?

Surviving The New Great Resignation: How To Create A World-Class Culture Your Employees Will Love

More and more stories about the comeback of the Great Resignation are appearing on our news feeds daily. Employers of every industry and every size are turning a worried eye to their own staff, wondering who among their ranks may be the next to hand in their two-week notice.

The good news is that there are things you can do *now* to help prevent a mass exodus of your top talent. As participation in the next Great Resignation increases, immediate action needs to be taken so that your employees aren't tempted to take part.

When my company, Berkshire Group Inc., was hired as a consultant by Human Arc, a healthcare service firm based in Cleveland, Ohio, there was no nationwide upheaval underway. However, their need to retain top talent to exceed financial and other goals was still very real.

Start With "Why?"

For Human Arc, the desire to create and implement a world-class company culture was based on increasing employee satisfaction and revenue, and affecting lives. The company was small, yet fast-growing, so it was an excellent time to create a culture from the ground up that would sustain the company for years to come.

Like Sinek implores us, always start by asking, "Why?" This is a crucial first step in the successful implementation of culture. Why do you want to do this?

A World-Class Culture—Built To Retain World-Class Talent

After meeting with Human Arc leaders and helping to form their strategic plan and core values, I continued to meet with them on a quarterly basis to ensure their goals remained on track. Sometimes those meetings were difficult. People had different opinions on how things should be done. The plan consisted of a set of innovative solutions to address company goals: employee retention, employee satisfaction, affecting lives, and increased revenue.

I introduced a leadership development program to train Human Arc's Leaders. The program included three Berkshire Group Inc. courses: Facilitation Training, Problem-Solving, and Everything DiSC for Leaders. Each program focused on equipping leaders with the skills to make them as effective as possible in their roles.

Your leaders determine your culture. How leaders are developed is critical to a company's success. The trainings provided leaders with the tools they needed to perform their roles with confidence, both up and down the chain.

Human Arc also invested in the Everything DiSC program for all associates. It was provided to every employee during the new-hire onboarding process. By helping employees understand their own communication style and how it interacts with those of their coworkers and leaders, it fostered stronger relationships across all levels of the organization, allowing for better communication and a much more comfortable working environment as a result.

Another system introduced to help with employee satisfaction was affectionately called "Applause." This online recognition system operated much like a social media platform, allowing Human Arc associates at all levels to create posts and award points to others to commend them for a job well done. The points could then be used to purchase items such as gift cards, jewelry, electronics, or even make donations to a chosen charity.

To be successful, employees need to know what is expected of them, how to meet those expectations, and what can be done to improve if they are not being met. Prior to the implementation of the strategic plan, Human Arc lacked an integrated system to track performance. Berkshire Group Inc. assisted in implementing a system that enabled leaders to outline goals for their direct reports clearly. This also equipped leaders with a tool to track progress and provide feedback to their direct reports for improvement.

Monthly meetings were conducted with the leadership team for the purpose of sharing information, furthering education, planning future steps, and celebrating wins. Cross-functional continuous improvement teams were formed and met regularly to address organizational issues and make recommendations. The leadership team also decided to share the company's financials with every employee. The information was made available on the public drive for all employees to view at any time. Being transparent about how the company was doing perpetuated further buy-in and the feeling of ownership.

The Result

After the successful implementation of the solutions provided by Berkshire Group Inc., Human Arc's culture evolved into one that associates were proud of. Turnover fell to an average of 20 percent. Employee satisfaction reached an all-time high. Human Arc was honored with winning the NorthCoast 99 award as a great place to work for fifteen years in a row, along with several other community service awards for their group volunteer efforts.

Thanks to the implementation of formal training, a focus on self-awareness, the introduction of systems, and transparency with company financials, Human Arc exceeded its revenue goals and continued to steadily grow its business. Developing people ultimately translates to business success.

Actions To Take

Communicate The Vision And Values Clearly And Often

A strong culture is built on shared understanding. Regularly articulate what success looks like, why it matters, and how each team member contributes to the bigger picture. Reinforce these messages in meetings, one-on-ones, and daily interactions.

Model The Culture You Want To Create

Leaders set the tone. Demonstrate the behaviors, values, and work ethic you expect from your team. Consistency in your actions builds trust and reinforces cultural expectations.

Hold Yourself And Others Accountable

Culture is not just about words; it's about action. Set clear expectations, provide feedback, and ensure alignment between stated values and actual behaviors. Recognize and reward behaviors that strengthen the culture while addressing those that undermine it.

Future Leadership Trends: Preparing For What's Coming

*Leaders of the future will have to be visionary
and be able to bring people in—real communicators.
These are things that women bring to leadership
and executive positions, and it's going to be incredibly
valuable and incredibly in demand.*
ANITA BORG

The most reliable way to predict the future is to create it.
OFTEN ATTRIBUTED TO ABRAHAM LINCOLN

The workplace is evolving faster than ever, and leadership must evolve with it. As we look to the future, leaders face new challenges and opportunities that require them to be more adaptable, empathetic, and forward-thinking than ever before. The following trends highlight what organizations must prioritize to develop leaders who can navigate the complexities of tomorrow's workplace.

Cultivating A Culture Of Continuous Learning

The pace of change in the modern workplace means that the skills leaders need today may become obsolete tomorrow. Organizations must embrace a culture of continuous learning, where leaders are encouraged—and expected—to develop new competencies throughout their careers. This isn't just about attending occasional workshops; it's about fostering a mindset of curiosity, adaptability, and growth.

Leadership development programs must integrate opportunities for ongoing learning in a variety of ways, including:

- Mentoring

- Coaching

- On-demand digital training

- Peer-to-peer collaboration

The most successful leaders will be those who view themselves not as finished products but as works in progress, always seeking to grow alongside their teams and organizations.

There may be a tendency to put continuous learning off to the side as we focus on running our teams and managing business growth. Investing in learning shores up our abilities as leaders and demonstrates to our team that improving our knowledge and skills never truly stops.

Equipping Leaders For Agility In The Evolving Workplace

The future of work demands leaders who can navigate ambiguity and adapt to constant change. Hybrid work models, global teams, and shifting employee expectations require leaders to develop agility, not just in their decision-making but in how they communicate, collaborate, and lead.

This includes teaching leaders how to:

- Effectively manage diverse and distributed teams

- Balance accountability with empathy in an increasingly flexible work environment

- Foster inclusiveness and trust in both in-person and virtual spaces

Agile leaders will need tools to manage change proactively while staying focused on long-term goals, ensuring their teams remain aligned and engaged even amid disruption. The ability to lead in this new landscape will not only determine the success of individual organizations but will also shape the broader future of work. Companies that invest in cultivating agile leaders will find themselves better positioned to innovate, retain top talent, and drive sustained growth. Leadership development programs must therefore evolve to include strategies that prepare leaders to thrive in uncertainty, empowering them to embrace challenges as opportunities.

Ultimately, the leaders who excel in this environment will be those who remain adaptable, empathetic, and forward-thinking. By equipping them with the skills and mindsets required to lead diverse, distributed teams and navigate the complexities of a hybrid world, organizations can ensure they are ready to meet the demands of tomorrow. The future of work is not just about adapting to change—it's about shaping it with intention.

Prioritizing Employee Wellness And Mental Health

The future workplace places a growing emphasis on employee wellness, and leaders are at the forefront of this shift. The pandemic brought mental health and work-life balance to the forefront of leadership priorities, and this focus isn't going away.

Leaders must develop emotional intelligence to recognize and address signs of burnout, stress, and disengagement. Beyond addressing immediate challenges, they should also create environments that proactively support well-being, such as the following:

- Flexible work arrangements

- Open communication channels that encourage psychological safety

- Initiatives that promote holistic wellness, including mental, emotional, and physical health

A healthy workforce is a productive workforce, and leaders who prioritize wellness will foster more engaged, loyal, and high-performing teams. By prioritizing employee wellness, leaders can create a ripple effect that extends beyond individual well-being to enhance team dynamics and organizational success. When employees feel supported and valued, they are more likely to bring their best selves to work, collaborate effectively, and contribute meaningfully to shared goals. This not only boosts productivity but also helps cultivate a workplace culture where innovation thrives.

As the future workplace continues to evolve, leaders who champion wellness will set a new standard for what it means to lead with purpose and compassion. They will not only help their teams navigate challenges but also inspire a deeper sense of commitment and trust. In doing so, these leaders will ensure their organizations remain competitive and relevant in an increasingly people-centric world.

Preparing For Rapid Technological Advances And The AI Revolution And Evolution

The next decade will bring unprecedented changes driven by rapid technological advancements, particularly in artificial intelligence (AI). Leaders must not only adapt to these changes but also anticipate their impact on the workforce, customer expectations, and organizational strategy.

Future leaders need to do the following:

- Understand how to integrate AI tools into their operations to improve efficiency and decision-making

- Anticipate how AI and automation may shift workforce needs and skill requirements

- Address ethical considerations related to AI, ensuring its use aligns with the organization's values

The leaders who succeed in this space will be those who view technology not as a threat but as an opportunity, leveraging AI and other innovations to empower their teams and improve organizational outcomes. As AI technology reshapes industries at an unprecedented pace, leaders who embrace a proactive and forward-thinking approach will be the architects of sustainable success. By aligning AI advancements with their organization's mission and values, they can unlock new opportunities while maintaining a strong ethical foundation. This balance will be critical in building trust among employees, customers, and stakeholders in an era of rapid change.

The leaders of tomorrow will be defined by their ability to navigate the complexities of AI integration with both strategic acumen and human-centric leadership. By fostering a culture of continuous learning, encouraging innovation, and addressing the evolving needs of their workforce, organizations can position themselves not just to adapt but to thrive. The future belongs to those who can harness the power of AI while keeping humanity at the core of their leadership.

Leading With Purpose And Empathy

As younger generations enter the workforce, they bring with them a desire for purpose and meaning in their work. Leaders must be able to connect their teams' daily efforts to the organization's larger mission, inspiring commitment and engagement.

Empathy will also be a critical leadership trait in the future. Understanding employees' diverse needs, challenges, and motivations will enable leaders to create authentic connections and foster a culture of trust. In an era of increasing automation, these human-centered skills will distinguish great leaders.

Leaders who prioritize purpose and empathy will be uniquely positioned to engage the next generation of talent. By linking individual roles to the organization's mission and demonstrating genuine care for their teams, they can achieve several results:

- Inspiring a deeper sense of belonging and motivation

- Boosting employee satisfaction

- Driving better performance

In short, people are more likely to excel when they feel valued and connected to a greater cause.

As workplaces continue to evolve, the most successful leaders will strike a balance between technological advancements and a human-centered approach. They will champion cultures that celebrate diversity, support growth, and nurture trust. By leading with authenticity and purpose, these leaders will not only meet the expectations of the modern workforce but also pave the way for a future where organizations thrive through shared vision and meaningful impact.

Building Leadership For The Future

The evolving workplace requires leaders to be learners, innovators, and role models for resilience and adaptability. Organizations that prioritize leadership and management development, equipping their leaders with the tools and skills to navigate these trends, will have a significant advantage in the future of work.

By embracing continuous learning, prioritizing wellness, leveraging technology, and leading with empathy, leaders can create workplaces where people thrive today and in the years to come.

Appendices

Acknowledgments

I am deeply grateful to Henry DeVries and Lisa Apolinski from Indie Books International for their invaluable process, unwavering support, and overall assistance. Your friendship and guidance mean the world to me.

To my daughter, Amanda: I couldn't be prouder of you. Beyond that, I am endlessly grateful for our deep conversations, your curiosity, and your desire to learn. In so many ways, you are a shining example of emotional intelligence, and I continue to learn from you.

A heartfelt thank you to my beta readers: your insightful feedback has been incredibly helpful in shaping this book. I also appreciate the encouragement and support from my network and community; your belief in me has been truly motivating.

Finally, to my clients over the decades: thank you. You challenge me, inspire me, and push me to keep growing so that I can continue to serve you at my best. I am honored to be part of your leadership journey.

About The Author

Janet Kendall White is the founder and CEO of Berkshire Group Inc., an award-winning, WBE- and WOSB-certified organization with a proven track record of transforming leaders, teams, and cultures for over three decades. A recognized expert in leadership development, Janet equips individuals and organizations with the tools, strategies, and insights they need to navigate challenges, communicate effectively, and achieve lasting success.

A sought-after speaker, facilitator, and executive coach, Janet has worked with leaders across industries—locally, nationally, and internationally—helping them elevate their leadership impact through strategic planning, coaching, and innovative assessment tools. Her expertise has been featured in *Entrepreneur, Fortune,* and *Bloomberg Businessweek*, and she has authored multiple training books designed to develop leadership skills in real-world environments.

Beyond her work with executives and organizations, Janet is deeply committed to serving her community. She has held leadership roles on numerous boards, including the National Association of Women Business Owners (NAWBO) Northeast Ohio chapter, the Stark State College Foundation, and the Cuyahoga Valley Association of Talent Development. She also dedicates time to supporting veterans through her role as scholarship coordinator for Rolling Thunder, Inc., Ohio Chapter 2.

When she's not coaching or speaking, Janet finds inspiration in the outdoors, often with her adult daughter, Amanda—whether cycling, hiking, kayaking, or exploring new landscapes. Her passion for leadership, resilience, and continuous growth is reflected in her work and her adventurous spirit.

This book is a culmination of her experience, offering actionable insights, proven strategies, and a fresh perspective on what it takes to become a truly resilient and effective leader.

Example Of Leadership Expectations
Taliaferro Project Guiding Principles

While discussing communication and expectations with Tom Taliaferro, Managing Director for People Consulting at Ernst & Young, LLP, he shared his personal guiding principles with me. While they might seem extensive, he works in an organization with almost 400,000 employees, and he wants all those who work with him to be clear about his expectations as a leader. I think it's a great example of leaving nothing to chance or assumption.

- Lead, follow, or get out of the way!

- Leadership comes from what we do and how we do it, not from a job or project title. Everyone can exhibit leadership.

- Leadership comes through the proactive combination of competence, courage, confidence, and compassion.

- Be confident in your actions and your responses.

- Use strong/action words and avoid soft words.

  - Avoid "I think," "kind of," "maybe," "sort of," "like."

  - Instead, use "is," "will," "know."

  - Avoid the phrase, "to be honest." It is assumed you are always honest. If the situation calls for it, use "to be direct" or "to be frank" instead.

- It is amazing what we can accomplish when we aren't worried about who gets the credit.

- Understand the purpose of your project, the higher purpose of the client, and try to embody this in how you interact with them:

  - What is the client's higher purpose?

    - What do they do?

    - Who do they serve?

    - Who are their customers?

    - What is their culture?

  - Try to understand what the personal win will be for your client counterpart and try to help them achieve it.

- Work hard; play hard.

- If you hoot with the owls, be ready to soar with the eagles!

- My door is always open, and there is no topic off limits for discussion.

- Be accountable to your work stream, deliverables, and budget; if you can't meet a deliverable, let the project manager know as soon as possible.

- Ambiguity is the enemy of accountability.

- I try to operate by the four pillars of trust:

  - Competent: relevant and effective knowledge, skills, abilities, and judgements

  - Open: open and honest in sharing information, plans, and decisions

  - Concerned: demonstrate caring about more than yourself

  - Reliable: inspire confidence by consistently producing what others expect

- Honesty and integrity are essential to maintaining that trust.

- If you have an issue, bring it to your project manager as soon as possible but be prepared to be asked for a recommended solution. Some things require a team discussion, so don't be afraid to speak up, but help be part of the solution.

- If you make a mistake, let the project manager know and don't try to cover it up. Everyone makes mistakes. It's how we resolve the mistake that makes the difference. Supervisors can't help communicate root cause if we are not aware, and root-cause analysis is part of helping us to communicate issues with the client. Project leadership will have your back if we are aware of the issue.

- If you make a mistake, call the project manager before calling the client.

- You don't need to ping me on Teams or text to ask if you can call me. If you ping me instead of calling, I assume it isn't urgent. Calling (cell or on Teams) is the most urgent way to contact me. Teams IM is the next most urgent way to reach me. I am rarely without my phone and usually only have it turned off when flying. I turn my phone ringer off at 10 pm and turn it back on at 6 am.

- When pinging with a question on Teams, go ahead and ask the question instead of typing my name and waiting for a response. I will put my DND on or log out of Teams if I'm not able to receive an IM.

- Timecards are required to be completed each week (fill it out ahead of time if traveling on a Friday). Put a recurring reminder on your calendar each week if you need to.

- If you will be out sick or attending a personal engagement and will be unreachable for a period of time, please notify me and your direct supervisor. (Note: Personal engagements are OK! We work long hours, and sometimes you can only do things during the workday. Just let us know if you are going to be out of touch for a while so I know in case something comes up.)

- If you don't have client conference calls and you are not working on-site with the client, I'm OK with flexible work schedules (subject to the item above that you are reachable).

- Email etiquette:

  - I tend to stay up on email and like to be responsive; if I can do it, so can you.

  - Try to check for follow-up emails in a thread before responding to the first email sent.

  - If you are unable to provide a response within four hours to an email, acknowledge that the email was received and give an indication of when you will have a response/answer.

  - If you are in an all-day meeting or workshop that will preclude responding to emails, put an out-of-office notice on indicating such

  - Avoid the email volley; if an item isn't resolved in three emails, schedule a call to discuss

- Project etiquette:

  - Review the scope of work and know what is in it. Be familiar with the scope, deliverables, budget, and roles and responsibilities.

  - Use of project tools and firm methodology is not an option.

  - Maintain all project documentation and artifacts in the project collaboration site. Check out, update, save, and check in documents rather than loading new documents with new versions. Do not keep the working/live copies of documents on your hard drives without having the most recent also on the collaboration site (hard lesson learned here).

o Show up to conference calls and meetings on time. I operate by the adage, "If you're not five minutes early, you are late" mentality (you can take the boy out of the Navy, but you can't take the Navy out of the boy). If you won't be on time, give the Project Manager a heads-up beforehand.

o Keep cell phones off the tables and on mute during meetings. Be present and don't multitask (I struggle with this one sometimes myself . . . call me out on it). 😊

o If you are leading a project meeting or call, show up prepared. If you are doing a virtual presentation, have it set up and be ready to share when the meeting starts. Don't get to the meeting and then launch the presentation.

o If you are presenting a PowerPoint or other type of presentation, practice your delivery before the meeting. Present the topic rather than reading each bullet.

o Status reports are required to be completed before the deadline day/time.

o Know what your budgeted hours are each week. If you don't know, ask the Project Manager for it. If you need to exceed your scheduled hours, let us know. If you don't exceed your hours one week, do not assume you can use them the following week without discussing with us; we may have to share unused hours with other work streams.

- ○ Know the client and your client counterpart. Know what the client's business is, what their culture is, and try to act as if you are an employee of the company. We should always dress similar to or better than the client.

- Help others when you have the availability. Ask others for help when you are overwhelmed.

- There is no such thing as a dumb question.

- Don't be afraid to tell me or the Project Manager when we are wrong.

- Don't be surprised if I challenge you on something. This isn't meant to be perceived as an attack or placing blame on something. It is often just to ensure the solution is solid and defendable and to help educate me so I can defend it to the client if/when the time comes if that is called for.

- When an issue is discovered, I will ask tough questions. But this is for root cause, not to place blame. Don't get defensive.

- *If we all follow the above items, we will have an extremely successful project and be rewarded accordingly!*

Works Cited And Author's Notes

1   HubSpot article, https://blog.hubspot.com/marketing/workplace-
    friendships (webpage no longer available), quoted in Holly
    Bengfort, "Employee Retention: The Real Cost of Losing an
    Employee," PeopleKeep, updated April 16, 2024, https://www.
    peoplekeep.com/blog/employee-retention-the-real-cost-of-losing-
    an-employee.

2   Hubspot article, quoted in Bengfort, PeopleKeep.

3   Chuck Mitchell et al., "C-Suite Outlook 2022: Reset and
    Reimagine," Conference Board, January 13, 2022, https://www.
    conference-board.org/publications/2022-reset-and-reimagine.

4   *Gallup's Employee Engagement Survey: Ask the Right Questions With
    the Q12® Survey*, Gallup, https://www.gallup.com/q12/.

5   Jim Harter, "Disengagement Persists Among U.S. Employees,"
    Workplace (blog), Gallup, updated September 11, 2023, https://
    www.gallup.com/workplace/391922/employee-engagement-
    slump-continues.aspx.

6   Chuck Mitchell et al., "C-Suite Outlook 2022."

7   Gallup, updated September 11, 2023.

8   Sandra Scharf and Kirsten Weerda, "How to Lead in a
    Hybrid Environment," *McKinsey & Company* (blog), June 27,
    2022, https://www.mckinsey.com/capabilities/people-and-
    organizational-performance/our-insights/the-organization-blog/
    how-to-lead-in-a-hybrid-environment.

9   Scharf and Weerda, "How to Lead in a Hybrid Environment."

10 Bonnie Dowling et al., "Hybrid Work: Making It Fit with Your
    Diversity, Equity, and Inclusion Strategy," *McKinsey Quarterly*,
    April 20, 2022, https://www.mckinsey.com/capabilities/people-
    and-organizational-performance/our-insights/hybrid-work-
    making-it-fit-with-your-diversity-equity-and-inclusion-strategy.

11 Jacquelyn Bulao, "How Fast Is Technology Advancing in 2024?,"
    TechJury, updated January 2, 2024, https://techjury.net/blog/
    how-fast-is-technology-growing/.

12 "The Great Exhaustion," McKinsey & Company, accessed May
    31, 2025, https://www.mckinsey.com/capabilities/people-and-
    organizational-performance/our-insights/five-fifty-the-great-
    exhaustion.

13 Steve Swavely, *Ignite Your Leadership: The Power of Neuropsychology
    to Optimize Team Performance* (Indie Books International, 2023).

14 Tim Templeton, *The Referral of a Lifetime: The Networking System
    That Produces Bottom-Line Results . . . Everyday!* (Berrett-Koehler,
    2003).

15 Michael Miller, "How Did the Pandemic Impact People's
    Emotional Intelligence?," Six Seconds, accessed June 1, 2025,
    https://www.6seconds.org/2021/06/23/pandemic-emotional-
    intelligence/.

16 Six Seconds, The Emotional Intelligence Network, *Emotional
    Intelligence Gaps Across the Generations*, Oct 26, 2021, https://
    www.6seconds.org/2021/10/26/emotional-intelligence-
    generations/.

17 Mahreen Khan, Amirali Minbashian, and Carolyn MacCann,
    "College Students in the Western World Are Becoming Less

Emotionally Intelligent: A Cross-Temporal Meta-Analysis of Trait Emotional Intelligence," *Journal of Personality* 89, no. 6 (2021): 1176–90, https://doi.org/10.1111/jopy.12643.

18 Madeleine A. Fugère, "Why Emotional Intelligence Is in Decline: Less In-Person Interaction, Lower Societal Empathy, and More," *Psychology Today*, November 13, 2021, https://www.psychologytoday.com/us/blog/dating-and-mating/202111/why-emotional-intelligence-is-in-decline.

19 Samantha Schwartz, "Meetings are shorter, but there's more of them in the pandemic," HR Drive, August 7, 2020, https://www.hrdive.com/news/virtual-meeting-work-hours-balance-pandemic/583208/?utm_source=chatgpt.com.

20 Kathryn Mayer. *HRE's Number of the Day: video meeting fatigue*, HR Executive, November 30, 2020, https://hrexecutive.com/hres-number-of-the-day-video-meeting-fatigue/.

21 Steven G. Rogelberg, "The Surprising Science Behind Successful Remote Meetings," MIT Sloan Management Review, May 21, 2020, https://sloanreview.mit.edu/article/the-surprising-science-behind-successful-remote-meetings/.

22 Mike Tolliver and Jonathan Sass, "Hybrid Work Has Changed Meetings Forever," *Harvard Business Review*, June 17, 2024, https://hbr.org/2024/06/hybrid-work-has-changed-meetings-forever.

23 Ruth Chang, "How to Make Hard Choices," TED Talk, New York, May 2014, posted June 18, 2014, by TED, YouTube, 14 mins., 41 sec., https://www.youtube.com/watch?v=8GQZuzIdeQQ&ab_channel=TED.

24 *Star Wars: Episode IV—A New Hope*, written and directed by George Lucas, 1977, Twentieth Century Fox.

25 Shaina Zazzaro, *Built By Resilience: Turn Every Setback Into Your Comeback* (Indie Books International, forthcoming).

26 Simon Sinek, *Start with Why: How Great Leaders Inspire Everyone to Take Action* (Portfolio, 2009).